Moving Past

The Death of a Loved One

Cindy Cipriani

abbott press®

A DIVISION OF WRITER'S DIGEST

Moving Past
The Death of a Loved One

Cover Design: Dr. Stanley El, D.Div.
Coaching: Mike Mataraza
Cover Photo: Jason Street

Abbott Press books may be ordered through booksellers or by contacting:

Abbott Press
1663 Liberty Drive
Bloomington, IN 47403
www.abbottpress.com
Phone: 1-866-697-5310

ISBN: 978-1-4582-0552-0 (sc)
ISBN: 978-1-4582-0554-4 (hc)
ISBN: 978-1-4582-0553-7 (e)

Library of Congress Control Number: 2012914119

Printed in the United States of America

Abbott Press rev. date: 11/08/2012

Dedication

I dedicate this book to all I have loved and lost:

Viola Letson	*(my Grandmother)*
Edith Rapp	*(my "Aunt E")*
John I & Lily Godshalk	*(my Grandparents)*
Robert & Dorothy Letson	*(my Uncle Bobbie & Aunt Dot)*
William Letson	*(my Uncle Bill)*
Jim & Pauline Letson	*(my Uncle & Aunt)*
Stanley Letson	*(my Dad-the best man ever)*
John Letson	*(my Uncle Johnie)*
Ada & H.A.Timmons	*(my Uncle Tim & his Ada-bird)*
Richard Letson	*(my Uncle Dick)*
Jack & Alice Keat	*(my cousins)*
Rosalia diGiacomo	*(my second mom)*
David Cipriani	*(my brother-in-law)*
Joseph & Ellen Cipriani	*(my in-laws)*
Joe & Mimi	*(my neighbors)*

To all who have helped, loved and encouraged me. And most of all, to God who looked in my heart, heard my prayers, inspired this writing and patiently guided me to put these thoughts on paper. Thank you for sending the dragonfly.

Moving Past
The Death of a Loved One

A Daily Guide & Journal
By Cindy Cipriani

Table of Contents

HOW TO USE THIS BOOK

Each chapter has a short introduction followed by daily readings. and a place to journal your thoughts. The daily readings contain a quote, comment and suggested activity to help guide your thoughts and emotions while processing your loss.

Journaling serves two purposes. First it can be a place to dump your feelings to relieve stress. Second, you will have a record of how you are progressing over time.

These readings are short intentionally so that you can take just a few minutes to read and then think about them throughout the day. You can turn to any chapter which corresponds to how you are feeling in the moment, and read something to help you understand and cope.

It is my wish that you never feel alone or abnormal throughout your grieving experience. Your life is different due to your loss, but you will find happiness and joy again.

My Story

One summer day in 2010, my heart was aching as I tried to figure out why my life had taken paths that I never would have anticipated. As I sat by the small fish pond in my back yard, I asked God to tell me what He wanted me to do with all the experiences of adversity and lessons I had learned from them. It was probably the first time I stopped asking for what I wanted or thought I needed, and asked Him what He wanted.

Suddenly a huge dragonfly flew by and landed on the back of the chair next to me. It sat there contentedly waving its wings slowly up and down. A long time passed and the dragonfly continued to keep me company. How odd, I thought. When I got up to go in the house, the dragonfly flew around me in a tight circle, and sat back down on the back of the chair. Startled, I realized that maybe I wasn't supposed to get up just yet. I sat back down and closed my eyes. Are you trying to tell me something God?

My thoughts raced back to when I was a teen. I thought I had my path completely figured out. I would graduate high school, get married, have 2.5 children, a dog, a beautiful house and become a full time minister in my religion. And that is what I did. At eighteen I married my high school sweetheart. We had two beautiful sons (and seeing how powerful the law of intention is – I endured a miscarriage in between, thus the .5) We worked hard and bought several homes, each one larger and more beautiful. And I spent most of my time in ministry work.

The truth was that while my path seemed right on track, it was just a façade. Behind the white picket fence in our yard, was an atmosphere of fear, anger, abuse and alcoholism. No one knew what truly went on behind closed doors. That is how I wanted it until the day when the pain of staying became greater than the fear of leaving. That decision made my life veer in a direction I had never anticipated. As the memories flowed I could feel the pain of being expelled from my religion, losing my family and friends, having no money, starting a business only to lose it after a car accident injured my back, having to sell my home and feeling so very alone and scared. Twice the pain was so overwhelming that I tried to end my life because I felt I had let everyone down, including God.

Besides all of that, I lost many loved ones in death throughout my lifetime. I was with many of them when they passed. I could see each of them now. God, why are you reminding me of all this pain? Why did I have to lose so many people that I loved? I could feel the heart ache and remember how each time was hard in a different way.

I wished I had a practical guide book that would have given me a hand to help me breathe through the painful moments and get me through each day. Life doesn't come with instructions, I thought. Remembering everything I have gone through and realizing how grateful I am now that I survived, I opened my eyes.

The dragonfly was still there watching me. I remembered my friend Jill once told me that if an animal strangely crossed my path, I should look up the Indian totem and find out what it was trying to tell me. So I immediately went to my computer and looked up dragonfly. This is a summary of what I found:

The dragonfly symbolizes a change in perspective of self realization, emotional and mental maturity and a deeper understanding of life. Its flight across the surface of the water represents looking deeper into the implications of life. The dragonfly can move in all six directions with power and poise – something that only comes with age and maturity. The iridescence of its wings is believed as the end of one's self created illusions and a clear vision into the realities of life. Also the discovery of one's own abilities by the unmasking the real self and removing doubts on your own identity.

Because the dragonfly lives most of its life as a nymph, it only is able to fly for a short time thus living IN the moment and to the fullest. By living in the moment you are aware of who you are, where you are, what you are doing, what you want, what you don't and can make informed choice on a moment-to-moment basis. This ability lets you live your life without regrets. Like the eyes of a dragonfly, who uses 80% of its brain for the ability to see, you can see beyond limitations into the vastness of the universe and your own capabilities.

Tears streamed down my face as I read. All the things I have been through had taught me lessons I needed to learn. Now I could see the deeper meaning and how I needed to spread my wings and fly forward without hesitation to help others. I was drawn to a box of writing that I had started years earlier. My hand seemed to know to pull out the file "Moving Past". I sat down at the computer and started to write.

If you ask me to quote from this book, I really can't. I don't feel like I was the one writing. The pages were downloaded to me and I transcribed them. My prayer is that this message with help you have a simple guidebook to help you through a difficult time, to know you aren't alone and to look for the signs that God puts in your path.

Write to me. I'd love to hear how this book has helped you.

-Cindy Cipriani

Part One
Breathing through the moments

Life is a journey of change. It can be wonderful and painful. Pain is often an opportunity for growth. But how?

While each person moves at a different pace, the process stays the same. Change brings – Shock, anger, hurt, despair, grief, strength and finally, growth. With each occurrence a small scar remains in our hearts as a reminder of the anxiety. When the next change happens, our memory of past change and how we negotiated it will surface and either help or hinder the speed of our adjustment to our new situation.

I have often asked why life has to be so hard. I longed for a simple guidebook to help walk me through a crisis; a reminder that others have gone through this and have come out on the other side. I needed something to read in the moment when I was having a hard time breathing. My bedside table became filled with books, but they were too deep, too intellectual to absorb. My eyes would read a few lines, and then I'd have to put it down because they were written from a clinical view. I just needed some quick advice or a thought to get me past the moment.

Having experienced moving past the death of over twenty very special people in my life, I wanted to create a guide book of daily readings that could be read quickly and give inspiration in the moment you need it most. This book is based on interviews with hundreds of people of varying ages, backgrounds and experiences. I have discovered that they all have experienced similar steps in the process of grieving, so I have formulated a process that I hope will help you in your journey.

Since you are unique, the 10 steps will occur differently for you than for anyone else. Each day may bring a different emotion in the process. This book is designed so that whatever you are feeling, you can turn to that chapter and read a passage that will help get you through the day. Don't think that anything is abnormal if your emotions jump around. That is normal. Everyone is different.

Often, you will experience a collision of several emotions all at once. You will have your unique formula of moving through this very hard time in your life. This book serves as a guide to clear your path by giving you a famous quote to ponder a thought for the day and then allow you to record your thoughts, emotions, actions and reactions so you can see your progress.

The pace that you move through the stages will vary. You may find yourself stuck. If that is the case, seeking professional counseling is the best way of releasing that emotion.

Be easy on yourself. Trust you are not alone. Everyone will experience loss and hardship in life. Moving past it may seem overwhelming at this moment. Just know you will smile again.

In short, let me give you some up front advice. Don't rush the process. Just know there is one, and you too can move through this very hard time and come out with strength, courage and wisdom.

After all, life is all about moving through and looking forward. The past has already happened, and the future is just a breath away.

How we deal with both is the only thing we can control.

Chapter 1

SHOCK – Deer In Headlights

NO MATTER HOW or why you have lost someone you love, it can be a shock to your system. You may find yourself repeating "I can't believe this is happening" over and over inside your mind. This is shock setting in. Shock is when you feel like you have been hit hard in the gut and your breath is taken away. You are stunned.

If you lost someone unexpectedly, shock may set in at the initial announcement. It doesn't matter if the news comes over the phone or in person, the words will throw your mind and heart into a world of disbelief and confusion. The world suddenly screeches to a halt and a time warp begins. You may feel your body moving, and you may hear words coming out of your mouth, but a part of your brain is now left in limbo. It is trying to reconcile the situation with reality, and during this time, reality is too painful to believe.

If you lose someone after a long or painful illness, you may experience feelings in a different order. You may try to prepare yourself for the inevitable as you support and care for the one who is ill. You may even experience relief when he or she finally stops breathing; because now they are no longer in pain or suffering. If this is the case, you may want to turn to the chapter that deals with Grief first. Grief can lead to despair; despair to anger; anger to hurt; and hurt to shock. Everyone is different in their reactions, so feel free to read the chapters in the order that you are experiencing the emotions for more immediate help. You may just need some guidance to readjust your life now that they are gone. In this case, turn to Part Two of this book.

In any case, be assured there is a reason for this disconnect between logic and acceptance. The neurotransmitters in your brain are trying to connect everything that you have been taught and have experienced, with this new change of circumstance. Your mind is short circuiting and causing a vacuum so that it can keep functioning without totally breaking down. This is a natural defense mechanism.

Some think that a strong belief system can help to ease the shock. But no matter what your beliefs are, death goes against our natural scope of understanding and reasoning. We realize that at some point everything dies. However, it goes beyond our natural ability to grasp that losing someone we love is "natural".

If you are a religious person, you have no doubt been taught that there is life beyond death. Some believe in reincarnation. Some believe in heaven. Even non-religious persons will confide that they hope there is some other place where we go after we die. But whatever your intellectual belief, your body's reaction turns to instinct when you lose someone you love.

> **As we approached her room in Intensive Care, I noticed the curtain was drawn. I immediately felt my stomach tighten and something deep inside knew that she was gone. A nurse stopped us and said, "I'm so sorry. Didn't anyone call you?" My hand covered my mouth as I gasped and I turned into my husband's open arms. I was shocked at how stunned I felt. Rosie was 103. For the last five years I told myself that she wouldn't live forever, but I still wasn't prepared for this moment. I wasn't ready to say goodbye to the**

woman who became like a mother to me. She was in such good health, and her mind was as sharp as a tack. We loved talking and laughing over dinner as she sipped her scotch on the rocks. Our friendship of thirteen years helped mould me into a better wife, mother and friend. I stood by her bedside unable to move. I wasn't ready to say goodbye.

Feeling like a deer in headlights is natural. Time stands still. All the unimportant details of life disappear. Immobility is your reaction to the most primal emotion – fear. You are entering unknown territory because suddenly your life has changed. All change is difficult, but here are a few things you can do when shock sets in:

1. Do what you need to do to say your personal goodbyes. Don't be rushed.

2. Turn to someone who isn't as emotionally attached to the person you have lost. They will be able to think more clearly in your hour of need. Let them act as a guide to what must be done, but don't allow them to tell you what you "should" be doing or feeling.

3. Know that everyone reacts differently. Don't judge your reaction; or that of others.

4. Take care of your physical body. Eat light food, drink plenty of water, and rest.

BONUS resource:

- This is from HelpGuide.org:
- Physical symptoms of trauma:

Grieving is normal following a traumatic event.

Whether or not a traumatic event involves death, survivors must cope with the loss, at least temporarily, of their sense of safety and security. The natural reaction to this loss is grief. Like people who have lost a loved one, trauma survivors go through a grieving process. This process, while inherently painful, is easier if you turn to others for support, take care of yourself, and talk about how you feel.

You can bring your nervous system back into balance by discharging this pent-up energy in a physical way:

- Trembling or shaking
- Sweating
- Breathing deeply
- Laughing
- Crying
- Stomach rumbling
- Feeling of warmth
- Goosebumps

Trauma self-help strategies:

Don't isolate. Following a trauma, you may want to withdraw from others. But isolation makes things worse. Connecting to others will help you heal, so make an effort to maintain your relationships and avoid spending too much time alone.

Ask for support. It's important to talk about your feelings and ask for the help you need. Turn to a trusted family member, friend, counselor, or clergyman. You may also want to join a support group for trauma survivors. Support groups are especially helpful if your personal support network is limited.

Establish a daily routine. In order to stay grounded after a trauma, it helps to have a structured schedule to follow. Try to stick to a daily routine, with regular times for waking, sleeping, eating, working, and exercise. Make sure to schedule time for relaxing and social activities, too.

Take care of your health. A healthy body increases your ability to cope with stress. Get plenty of rest, exercise regularly, and eat a well-balanced diet. It's also important to avoid alcohol and drugs. Alcohol and drug use can worsen your trauma symptoms and exacerbate feelings of depression, anxiety, and isolation.

When to seek professional help for emotional or psychological trauma:

Recovering from a traumatic event takes time, and everyone heals at his or her own pace. But if months have passed and your symptoms aren't letting up, you may need professional help from a trauma expert.

It's a good idea to seek professional help if you're:

- Having trouble functioning at home or work
- Suffering from severe fear, anxiety, or depression
- Unable to form close, satisfying relationships
- Experiencing terrifying memories, nightmares, or flashbacks
- Avoiding more and more things that remind you of the trauma
- Emotionally numb and disconnected from others

Trauma disrupts the body's natural equilibrium, freezing you in a state of hyper arousal and fear. In essence, your nervous system gets stuck in overdrive. Successful trauma treatment will address this imbalance and reestablish your physical sense of safety.

DAILY READING

> **"The trouble with quotes about death is that 99.999 percent of them are made by people who are still alive."**
> **– Joshua Bruns**

Losing someone you love is one of the most difficult emotional trials that your heart will endure. Time seems to slow to an unbearable pace. Your brain tries to think normal thoughts, but all the small details of life that always seemed so important, don't even come to mind. The air feels like a thick broth which makes your movements heavy and draining. Over and over your mind may keep repeating, "Why? . . . . How can this be happening? . . . .Why? . . . .

How will I get through this?"

It is okay to feel stunned. Your mind and body are protecting you from immediate emotional harm. Today, tell yourself that you will be okay. Tell yourself that today you need rest, and your mind is resting as it prepares to handle the feelings to come.

Now, rest. Find a place to sit and stare. It's okay.

Write down how you are feeling. Journal your journey:

_____

_____

_____

_____

_____

_____

_____

_____

_____

_____

_____

_____

_____

_____

_____

_____

_____

_____

_____

_____

DAILY READING

> **"This existence of ours is as transient as autumn clouds. To watch the birth and death of beings is like looking at the movements of a dance. A lifetime is a flash of lightning in the sky. Rushing by, like a torrent down a steep mountain."**
>
> **-Buddha**

There are things to do to prepare to say goodbye. There are people to notify, places to go, decisions to be made. Life is moving forward, but your heart is stuck in the moment your loved one left. You make the calls, go to the places, and make the decisions, while feeling like your soul is somewhere else. Your body is robotically doing what is necessary. You will make sure the arrangements are perfect in their honor.

It is natural to want the best for your loved one. Today think of them, and who they were and how they would want to be honored. Perform a ritual in their honor to help you let go.

They will love whatever you do for them.

Write down what you did today, and how you are feeling.

_____

_____

_____

_____

_____

_____

_____

_____

_____

_____

_____

_____

_____

_____

_____

_____

_____

_____

_____

_____

DAILY READING

> **"The bitterest tears shed over graves are for words left unsaid and deeds left undone."**
> *- Harriet Beecher Stowe*

The ritual of saying farewell is meant to pay tribute to those you love. Viewings and funerals are occasions to reminisce, comfort and be comforted. No matter how perfect your personal relationship with the one who has passed has been, today your goodbye will feel too final, and too soon. You may start to regret leaving things unsaid. Whether there were words of love or of resentment, it is now too late to reconcile. Your mind is melting the shock, and the hurt is starting to puddle in your chest.

This has been a hard day. Again, you need to give yourself permission to rest. Force yourself to eat small meals, hydrate yourself after all the tears. Curl up and sleep.

Note the highlights of the day (people who came, words that warmed you, flowers or gifts that showed love, anything you remember from the service, and how your emotions carried you through the day).

DAILY READING

**"There is no greater sorrow than to recall
in misery the time when we were happy."**
- Dante

Numbness has been your friend. It has come to shield you from the pain of reality.

Now reality hits like an unwelcome knock at the door. As you swing the door open, the enemy stares deep into your soul. You stare back, not able to change the dark circles under your eyes, the sad frown or the slump of your shoulders. Reality takes off the veil of protection, and the pain greets you.

Remember how strong you are. You have experienced pain before, although different. It will not defeat you. The hurt is just your awareness returning to normal. Take special care of your body today. Again, nourish yourself with water to rehydrate. Rest. Hug a pet. Animals instinctively know you are suffering. They can make the best friends at times like this.

Write down your random thoughts. Don't analyze. Just record.

_____

_____

_____

_____

_____

_____

_____

_____

_____

_____

_____

_____

_____

_____

_____

_____

_____

_____

_____

_____

Chapter 2

HURT – Emotional and Physical

ACTIVITY CAN MASK the depth of your pain. After all, there was so much to do to get through the formalities of saying good- bye.

Whether you felt like you had to put on a brave face, or spent the first few days sobbing, the sudden quietness after everyone else leaves can feel like a giant vacuum of loneliness. People hug, smile, give their condolences, and then return to their lives. Their life goes on.

Your world stops beating, and the reality of your loss can come like a wave of hurt. Slowly your mind has been releasing the shock and allowing your emotions to embrace the pain. There can be a hollow pit in the center of your chest that feels like it could collapse and your whole being will be sucked into the void. Every muscle hurts from head to toe. The weight of breathing is exhausting.

The physical pain is a result of the stress that your muscles have been holding throughout the shock stage, and the initial adrenalin you produced to get through that time. You probably weren't even aware how much energy you needed when in survival mode. Now, your body is in need of recovery literally and emotionally.

The healing process of your literal body will be shorter than healing the hurt of your loss, if you take care of yourself during this time. Sometimes the hurt can come upon you suddenly, as if your tolerance threshold has been filling up and reaches a point where it overflows.

> When my father died, I thought my mother was in denial. She went about her daily activities like nothing happened. Until one night weeks after the funeral, she excused herself from the table, walked in her bedroom, closed the door and began to wail and sob with a pain that I had never heard before.

Stress lowers your metabolism. It can also cause other issues such as insomnia, over eating, under eating, increase in alcohol or smoking consumption. All of these factors will take a toll on your well being. The more worn down you become, the harder it will be to combat the pain of your loss.

Using natural oils, like the Star of Bethlehem can ease grief, sadness and trauma. Simple breathing exercises can increase the flow of oxygen which will calm and revitalize your body. Taking three deep breaths and letting them out slowly, recharges your body and calms your spirit.

BONUS resource:

- Nutritional Supplements Guide.com

Vitamins for Stress

One effective method of stress relief management involves the use of vitamins. Taking in extra nutrients helps to ensure that the body will have adequate amounts in store to combat stress. Among the most important stress vitamins are the B-complex vitamins and the antioxidant vitamins.

B-complex vitamins are important in stress relief management because one of their primary roles in the body is to keep the nervous system functioning well.

Deficiencies of B-vitamins are associated with nerve problems and an increase in stress-related symptoms such as depression, anxiety and irritability. The B-complex vitamins work as a team, and supplements should include a balanced formula containing all of them.

Vitamins E and C, both antioxidants, protect the body against free radical damage. When the body is under stress, more free radicals are produced, so extra antioxidants can be of great value. Antioxidants also help to strengthen the immune system, which can be compromised during stressful times.

Nutritional supplements for stress relief management should contain more than vitamins. Several minerals and herbs are of value in combating the effects of stress as well.

For example, the minerals magnesium and zinc are often depleted when a person is under stress, and supplements may help to replenish stores and alleviate stress-related symptoms. In addition, herbs can be used to treat a variety of stress-related conditions.

Often people go to the doctor and get prescription anxiety medications to get through the death of a loved one. While I am not a medical professional, and you should consult and take the advice of a trusted doctor, I can say that people have reported that these medications can help get you through the stress of the first few days or weeks. Having said that, doctors caution long term usage. You should also make sure to talk to your doctor about side effects such as weight gain, sleeplessness, stomach and intestinal problems and added anxiety. Psychiatrists, Mental Health Professionals and General Practitioners recommend using these medications in conjunction with counseling to address not only the physical effects of grief, but the emotional and psychological ones.

Before turning to medications, you may want to try speaking to a trusted friend or relative, simple breathing exercises, or even going for regular walks. Physical activity will help your body to calm both the physical anxiety as well as the sad thoughts you are carrying. If you do ultimately decide to use medication, doing these things has been reported to help more than medication alone.

At times it is more comfortable to speak to a professional than someone you know. In our society we are often told not to cry. Well meaning people may tell you that "this too will pass". They even will say hurtful things without realizing it. Those with religious beliefs might say things like, "It was their time" or "They are in a better place now". While seeming like comforting things to say, to you it can be like rubbing salt in a wound. They can go back to their normal lives as if nothing happened, while you are left to wallow in the pain of loss and loneliness. Even though people die every day, it is totally different when it is someone that has made your life better just by knowing them. They leave a void that hurts.

The void is not just because the person is not with you anymore. It is for the unfulfilled plans and dreams that you had with that person. Death often makes you recall others you have lost in the past. Right now it may seem that no one else feels the depth of loss as you do. You may want to withdraw from people so as to avoid having to put on a false smile or hear one more person say how sorry they are. But withdrawing is not advisable. Remember that others are mourning too. They do not know how you are feeling, and may not know what to do or say to help you. But don't take this as a sign that they are fine, or that they don't care about you. Reach out to your loved ones and do for them what you need yourself. You will be helping everyone, including yourself.

Moving Past

Many who have lost their spouse or their child have expressed that the most helpful thing they did when the hurt was overwhelming was to talk to someone who had suffered a similar loss. Although everyone feels differently, there are common emotions that can be shared and there is a sense of relief that they understand without your explaining. If you can't locate a specific grief support group in your area, ask your friends, coworkers or family if they know someone who you could talk to who has been through a similar loss.

<u>Things to Do When You are Hurting:</u>

- Spend time with a pet – they love you unconditionally and can provide love and comfort
- Write 10 to 15 minutes daily – Journaling helps get out whatever you are feeling without being censored
- Sit still and focus on breathing – This calms the soul and refreshes your body; you are probably holding your breath more than you realize
- Housecleaning – Put your mind on tasks that need to be done; the exercise will also help
- Exercise – Walking, Running, Stretching
- Yoga – Join a class or get a video
- Crafts or hobbies – Occupies your mind; creates a feeling of enjoyment and accomplishment
- Friends – laugh, cry, express anger
- Find a Support Group-when friends and family have gone back to their normal lives a support group can provide the understanding you need.

DAILY READING

> **"'Pain' is the fundamental human predicament. No one escapes life without experiencing pain, although many become preoccupied with attempts to alleviate it.**
>
> **Pain is the overriding, inexplicable condition of life...the touchstone of our lives. In this 'trysting place', heaven and earth meet. Here we meet each other in humanity.**
>
> **And, more important, God meets us."**
>
> **-Edward Kuhlman**

You may think of a "tryst" as a meeting place for lovers. A place of anticipation and longing. However, the tryst that Sir Kuhlman speaks of is a meeting place called pain, for humanity and God. While all of humanity experiences pain, does God? Does God understand the depths of your soul's grief? You may start to question why this loss was allowed to happen. Why did God "take" your loved one? Trying to make sense of the loss is like putting the pieces of a puzzle together.

Your logical side tells you that everyone dies at some time. Your emotional side realizes that if you had the power, you would have changed what happened. Your physical side aches to understand. Your spiritual side feels guilty that you are even asking to understand. All of these powerful beliefs collide in a wide spectrum of confusion, faith, and human frailty.

No matter what your spiritual or religious convictions, talk to your Higher Power today. Pour out your heart.

Record what you need answers to.

_____

_____

_____

_____

_____

_____

_____

_____

_____

_____

_____

_____

_____

_____

_____

_____

_____

_____

_____

DAILY READING

> **You see sir; death is an intellectual matter, but dying is pure pain.**
> **- John Steinbeck**

Your instincts protect you from pain. When you touch something too hot, your hand quickly pulls away. When you feel threatened, you run away. Emotionally, pain comes without an invitation. This pain is deep inside your gut. You can't run from it. You can't avoid it. As the shock wears off, and the hurt of loss starts to wave over you, you have two choices. One is to try to mask the pain. The other is to curl into a ball and hold on to yourself as you rock yourself to sleep.

Masking the pain with alcohol, drugs, sex, violence, work, or food will only prolong the hurt. It is normal to want to avoid the agony. But it must be faced. Just as when you have literally hurt yourself, healing takes time. The initial pain of the injury goes away before the wound is thoroughly healed. But be reassured that the pain does diminish with time.

Read this out loud: Today I will allow myself to feel the pain of my loss. I will hug myself and treat myself kindly. I will remember that my hurt means that I loved. That love will never die.

Record what pain you are feeling: Mentally, Emotionally, and Physically.

_____

_____

_____

_____

_____

_____

_____

_____

_____

_____

_____

_____

_____

_____

_____

_____

_____

Record how you will comfort yourself.

_____

_____

_____

_____

_____

_____

_____

_____

_____

_____

_____

_____

_____

_____

_____

_____

DAILY READING

The pain is unrelenting; one does not abandon, even briefly, one's bed of nails, but is attached to it wherever one goes.
- William Styron

The days move forward. No one can see your bed of nails. Yet it is there, right beneath your skin. Guarded you move through time trying not to show the hurt. When you smile, the nails scratch at you. If you dare laugh, the nails pierce your heart. Your head aches trying to align the light moments of life with the pain and guilt of loss. You wonder if you will ever be able to not feel so hollow, if other people will ever not seem so shallow.

This is the normal process of grief. It will pass, but slowly. Remember that as you pass strangers on the street, or your loved ones in the kitchen, some of them are also carrying their bed of nails. You just can't see theirs. So be kind and gentle. Smile a small greeting. You never know who you just helped through the day. Plus, it will help you to remember you aren't alone in this journey of life, and loss.

Read out loud: Today I will look around for others who have that distant look in their eye. I will remember that there are others who are suffering. I will greet them with a look of understanding and empathy.

_____

_____

_____

_____

_____

_____

_____

_____

_____

_____

_____

_____

_____

_____

_____

_____

_____

_____

DAILY READING

And I look again towards the sky as the raindrops mix with the tears I cry.
- Unknown

In times of sorrow, rainy days can provide the background you need to just let it all out. A good hot shower will do the same.

Just when you think there must not be one more tear left in your dehydrated body, out of nowhere tears flow again. It may be something simple, like a song that plays on the radio on your way to work that automatically reminds you of your loved one. You may think you see him or her in a crowd. Someone laughs in the distance, and it sounds just like them. All of these memories cause tears because your emotions are so raw. Unfortunately in our society, crying is uncomfortable to some, especially for men. Growing up how many times did someone tell us to, "Stop crying."

My dad used to say about crying, "That is why God gave us tear ducts." I was very fortunate to grow up with an emotionally sensitive man. He would cry while watching Lassie rescue the little boy from the well, when leaving his sick mother-in-law's bedside, and when standing beside the coffin of someone he loved. He was one of the strongest men I have ever known, and his crying was a wonderful lesson in dealing with the pain of loss, or the happiness of relief.

Crying is a release valve for the soul, just as a tea kettle blows off steam when boiling. Let no one condemn your tears, including yourself. If you haven't been able to cry, ask yourself why.

Then go out in the rain and look up.

Ask yourself: How do I feel about crying and showing my sadness? Why?

_____

_____

_____

_____

_____

_____

_____

_____

_____

_____

_____

_____

_____

_____

_____

_____

_____

_____

_____

DAILY READING

The death of a friend is equivalent to the loss of a limb.

- German Proverb

Losing a limb is life changing. All the things you could do before and not even think about have to be changed to accommodate the missing limb. There are remarkable stories of those who have come back from war, survived car accidents, and overcome disease, which have learned to move through life with their new bodies. Adaptation is the key. They learn to think and move differently. Often they will "feel" the missing appendage. Doctors say this is because the mind remembers the sensation that the nerves used to have that were attached to that part of the body.

Losing a loved one is similar in that you too have to think and move through life differently now. Places that were familiar to the two of you, will now feel empty. Routinely picking up your cell phone to text them will suddenly remind you that they aren't going to respond.

Like losing a limb, it will take time and practice to be able to replace usual moments with new ones. Can you imagine how hard it would be to try to eat with a spoon held in your opposite hand? How difficult would it be to build up the muscles in your arms to push your wheelchair all day? These physical disabilities can only be overcome by being determined to build the strength and endurance that is necessary.

What ways of coping can I practice? What every day activities need to be replaced with a new way of being? How am I comfortable communicating with my lost loved one?

_____

_____

_____

_____

_____

_____

_____

_____

_____

_____

_____

_____

_____

_____

_____

_____

_____

_____

DAILY READING

It is hard to have patience with people who say There is no Death or Death doesn't matter. There is death. And whatever is matters.
-C.S.Lewis

"This too shall pass". "He's in a better place now." "They have moved on to another life form." "They will always be in your heart." "It was her time." Well intentioned people may give you their opinion on life and death. Does it make you angry when they say something that makes it seem like death is just something that happens? Sure, logically we know that everything eventually dies. But who can be logical right now? No, right now emotion has a checkmate on logic. You have probably said similar things to someone else in an attempt to be comforting. However, now you can see how empty these attempts are.

Remember that anger is normal. Remember they are only trying to help. Forgive their inability to read your emotions. Write down some things that would help, so you can remember to say them to someone else in the future. Remember that saying nothing, but doing something is always a good thing. Don't get stuck on these comments or people. Feel what you feel. Believe what you believe.

Ask yourself: What can I do next time someone loses a loved one that would make them feel better?

What should I say or not say?

How can I let them know that what they are feeling matters?

_____

_____

_____

_____

_____

_____

_____

_____

_____

_____

_____

_____

_____

_____

_____

_____

_____

_____

_____

Chapter 3

ANGER – What do I do with this?

WHEN UNDER ENOUGH pressure, eventually something will explode. It is a reaction to pressure.

When you can't take any more emotionally, you can explode with anger. Death is unfair, unacceptable, and unbelievably painful, no matter what the circumstances.

It is normal to become angry. You may direct that anger at God, at a doctor, at the person who caused the accident, even at yourself for not being able to stop it from happening. Whenever something is out of our control (which all of life really is but we pretend it isn't), we can become angry due to the frustration of an outcome that we don't want.

Anger can be a wonderful release of tension that has built up in our body. However, if it is misdirected, it can make the healing process much worse.

> For example, when Sean's daughter accidently died in a skiing accident, his first reaction was to go to the local bar and have a few drinks. The man sitting next to him reached for the bowl of peanuts in front of him, and he exploded yelling that it was HIS bowl of peanuts and how dare the guy steal them from him? A fight pursued, and Sean found himself in jail. His anger was misdirected to a stranger who thought he was crazy, when really he was angry at having his daughter taken from him in such a tragic, unexpected and unfair way.

People have been known to break something that was owned by the deceased, only to regret that later. The anger stage of loss is definitely a dangerous time if left to get out of control. In therapy, many doctors allow their patients to pound on a pillow, or scream into one, to release the pent up feelings. Under a controlled environment, exercises like this can help you. Speaking with a priest, minister or trusted friend will also help keep the anger from getting out of control. Anger can come up suddenly and take you by surprise. You may find yourself lashing out at people or becoming angry over little things, like dropping a pencil. This anger is a prelude to experiencing the pain and despair of loss. It is natural, but needs to be controlled to keep you safe and moving forward in your loss.

Anger will come and go throughout the process of grieving. Your emotions will be all over the place. If you find you have lashed out unexpectedly, apologize. The person who took the lashing may not understand where it came from, but your apology will be appreciated.

All anger stems from hurt. When we are hurt, our natural defenses rise up in protest. When someone is ripped from us, it hurts. It hurts badly. The more we hurt, somewhere along the line, an equal amount of anger will appear. It may come immediately after the shock because you don't want to acknowledge how hurt you are. The pain becomes arduous, so you might lash out at people. They can't see the agony that you are holding in your gut, so they just think you are out of line. Their anger may flare in response. Your words or actions, although unintentional, may cause them hurt resulting in their anger.

You may find yourself angry because you didn't get to say goodbye. Or maybe it is because the relationship you had will now never be different. Often if you lose someone that you didn't really get along with or didn't really understand, you get angry about the relationship that should have been. Like when a daughter loses her mother who she didn't see eye to eye with. In her mind she may think that their relationship should have been more loving. Now it is frustrating to think that there is nothing she can do to have the relationship she always wanted.

This is a dangerous time. People tend to act irrationally when they are angry. They do destructive things to themselves, objects or others. Be especially aware of your actions when the anger starts to well up in you. Drinking too much, getting into arguments, destroying something or acting out will only cause you to fall deeper into grief. Anger usually doesn't last long. The results of anger, last forever.

What can you do? It is alright to be angry. Anger is an emotion that we were given, just like all the others. It is a release of feelings. It is a purging of pain. Controlled anger is the key. Tell those around you how you are feeling. Let them know it has nothing to do with them. Get their support and help to take out this feeling in a healthy way. Friends don't let friends go ballistic. Friends don't let friends take revenge. Friends will protect you from yourself during this time.

Have someone you can call at 3am when you are pacing around the house like a caged lion. Hit a pillow instead of a wall. Don't break anything that belonged to your loved one. That may seem strange, but often you think you are just mad at the situation, but you can be mad at your loved one for leaving you. Even though you know they had no choice

36

in the matter, you can still get mad at them. If your parent has just died, you can feel like an orphan even though you are a grown adult. If your spouse has died, you can feel like they left you to face the world on your own. If your child has passed, you may not be able to mentally accept that they are gone before you are. How dare they leave you?

How dare God take them from you? No matter how spiritual or religious you may be, being angry at God will be natural too. Even those who claim to have no belief in a higher power, get mad at God for not being there. I have seen staunch atheists get mad at God after losing a loved one. How can that be? It is their way of trying to reconcile something that is unnatural, unfair and painful. Churches will tell you that this is the time you need God the most. But it may feel just the opposite. If you are a believer, remember that God gave you this emotion of anger. He also gave you the opportunity to pray. So go ahead and yell at God. He can take it. The Bible is filled with men and women who wept and cried out to him in grief. It can really help to release the anger.

The danger can be to stay mad too long. A few days of anger is normal and can be expected. Anger may come here and there during the day when you are under stress or when you are tired or not taking care of yourself. This is normal. But if you continue in an angry state day after day for more than a few days in a row, seeking the help of a grief counselor or minister is in order. Why?

Remember that all anger is caused by hurt. Anger masks the hurt. The longer you mask the hurt, the more hurt will build and the longer it will take to let go. Hurt can lead to despair; despair can make you angry; this merry-go-round is not healthy and will keep you stuck in your grief.

Realize that anger is a natural part of the grieving process. Be aware of how much and how long this emotion is residing in you.

Have a plan to move past the anger so you can feel the hurt. Yes, you must feel the hurt before you can begin to move past your pain.

DAILY READING

> **Bestrew the heart that makes my heart to groan.**
> **- William Shakespeare**

To call evil down upon the heart of someone who makes you ache may happen verbally or deep inside your subconscious. You may be angry at your loved one for leaving you. An abandoned dog will act afraid and often growl and bark at the person who is trying to help them. They have been hurt, and are afraid of being hurt again, even though they know they desperately need help. At times this anger comes and goes throughout the day. At times it stays around like a dark shadow that follows you everywhere. This anger is actually a sign that you are progressing through your grief. Your emotions are opening up, allowing your energy to fight for your survival.

Read out loud: Today when I'm feeling angry, I will embrace it. I have a right to be angry. I have just lost someone I love, and it isn't fair. If I take out my anger in an inappropriate way on someone else, I will apologize and let them know I'm not angry at them. I will tell them I am dealing with a loss, and I will seek a place of safety where I can yell into space and free my inner emotions.

Record how your anger manifests itself and how you dealt with it:

_____

_____

_____

_____

_____

_____

_____

_____

_____

_____

_____

_____

_____

_____

_____

_____

_____

_____

_____

DAILY READING

> **Take this sorrow to thy heart, and make**
> **it a part of thee, and it shall nourish thee till**
> **thou art strong again.**
> **- Henry Wadsworth Longfellow, "Hyperion"**

Pleading with your Higher Power to take your sorrow and store it in His heart until you are strong again is one way to hurt a little less. You may not be able to understand the "whys" of what has happened, but physically you need to move forward to get back to your daily routine. Visualizing that you have entrusted your pain with someone or something stronger than yourself can allow you to get work done, chores accomplished and thank you notes written. However, this is only a temporary reprieve.

As soon as you pause during the day, or lay down at night, your hurt can return. He will give it back to you so that you can start to cope by yourself. Like building a muscle, the soreness made by exercise is a sign that you are getting stronger. Keep asking for help in dealing with the uncomfortable feelings. Keep reassuring yourself that you are allowed to be sad.

Read out loud: Today, I will hand my sorrow over to my Higher Power. I will ask him to hold it next to his heart, and to give it back to me a piece at a time so that I can cope with it. Each day I will become stronger. Each day will get better.

Write your definition of your Higher Power and how you feel when you can entrust your grief to Him.

_____

_____

_____

_____

_____

_____

_____

_____

_____

_____

_____

_____

_____

_____

_____

_____

_____

_____

_____

_____

DAILY READING

**Always do what you want, and say what you
feel, because those who mind don't matter,
and those who matter don't mind.**
- Dr. Suess

Who is Theodore Geisel? Odds are you have no idea. However, chances are you have read and re-read many of his books. Theodore Geisel is Dr. Suess. On his way to obtaining a Ph.D. in classical literature, he decided to travel through Europe looking for inspiration. During his quest, he started writing poems and drawing silly characters. How would he have known that those sketches and simple statements would become the teaching tools of millions who are learning to read? "The Cat in the Hat" is a classic.

The reason they work so well is that he took a complicated idea and broke it down to simplicity. I'm sure there were many of his friends and family who told him he was crazy to be writing these silly books. But he listened to his inner wisdom, and just kept toiling over his ideas. His characters are so strange because he never learned to draw. His cars and houses defy gravity and logical rules. That is what makes them so fun.

At times when we feel the most confused with life, we often find a hidden wisdom lying in the mess. Just when life feels like nothing makes sense, try to boil it all down to the simplest form and accept that sometimes life doesn't follow the rules of logic.

Follow your instincts. Do what you want, say what you feel. Notice who is supportive, and who tells you that you are crazy. Those who truly love who you are won't mind the diversion from sanity.

Today, try something you have always wanted to do but have been too conservative to try.

I'm going to:

_____

_____

_____

_____

_____

_____

How it felt:

_____

_____

_____

_____

_____

_____

_____

_____

DAILY READING

Let us not look back in anger, nor forward in fear, but around in awareness.
– James Thurber

When you are truly still, you become aware of the moment. We spend so much of our life reliving the past, or worrying about the future. It may be really hard to be in this moment.

When you look back at what happened to take your loved one away, deep inside you may feel the burning sensation of your stomach acids churning. Often your emotions upset your gastrointestinal system. It wasn't something you ate, or a bug you picked up off a doorknob. No, you just could be angry.

Looking forward is too difficult right now. There were so many things you wanted to do, say and share with them. The fear of a future that is so different than you planned can also sour your gut. You may think you just aren't feeling well, but that gas and cramping could be your body saying, "Hey...something is wrong. My equilibrium is off. There are a bunch of pent up emotions that got stuck down here."

So, how can you deal with this moment? The moment when you realize that you have feelings that you don't know how to deal with? Well, if you did have a bug, you would take some medicine. If you ate something bad, you would drink a lot of water, and lay down to sleep allowing your body to flush the poisons out of your system. The same can be done now. Be aware of what your body needs to support the mess of emotions that it may be trying to hold back.

Your anger needs medicine – a good cry, a talk with a friend, or a long walk. Your fear needs attention - advice from someone who has moved past this time of grief to help you imagine that the future will be different, but it will be okay.

What is my body feeling?

_____

What am I holding in?

_____

Who can help me move past the anger and fear?

_____

Am I getting the rest I need?

_____

DAILY READING

Anger is not only inevitable, it is necessary. Its absence means indifference, the most disastrous of all human failings.
- Arthur Ponsonby

When you don't truly care one way or the other about someone, your emotions are usually passive as well. In order to have a strong reaction such as anger, you must have cared. In anger, people will often shout, "I don't care!" But just the energy that the outburst took shows you actually do care.

Indifference when you love someone, is just the plunger pushing down your emotions deep into your gut where they will ferment until someday when they will come exploding out mentally or physically. Allow your feelings of anger, grief and sadness to dissipate as they come. Allow the steam of your boiling emotions to be released in a healthy way.

How much do I care that my loved one is gone?

_____

_____

_____

_____

_____

_____

_____

_____

_____

_____

_____

_____

_____

_____

_____

_____

_____

_____

_____

DAILY READING

*An emotional circle – Anger comes from Hurt
of Grief; Grief can lead to Despair; Despair can
make us Angry. This circle masks our fear.*
— *Cindy Cipriani*

When an animal senses danger, it goes into defense mode. It stands perfectly still in order to hear any sound of an approaching enemy. The hair on its back stands up to exaggerate its size. It gets ready to fight.

When we are hurt, confused and fearful after the death of a loved one, our animal instincts kick in. Adrenaline stimulates the tiny muscles at the base of each hair follicle, collectively called the *arrector pili*, which pulls our hair upright. We stand taller and get ready to attack anyone verbally who reminds us of our pain, because we don't quite know how to act right now.

How am I expressing my hurt, bitterness and grief?

_____

_____

_____

_____

_____

_____

_____

_____

_____

_____

_____

_____

_____

_____

_____

_____

_____

_____

_____

_____

Chapter 4

DESPAIR – Breathe In and Out

IF YOU TURNED directly to this chapter, consider this a huge hug. It is at this stage that most people do reach out to find something that will help pull them out of the dark, bleak cavern of despair that has enveloped them. Please know that you are not alone, even though it feels like you are the only person in the world who has ever felt this kind of emotional pit.

Some experts call this stage of grief "bargaining". Bargaining is a time when you would do anything if this pain would be taken from you.

Everyone has felt despair at one time or another. Yes, everyone. You could stop anyone on the street, and ask them if they have suffered a loss and they would answer Yes. Repeat this to yourself…Everyone has felt despair and they have moved past it. I can too. But how?

Think back to other times in your life when you have experienced difficult circumstances. How did you move through them? Perhaps you lost a pet as a child, or broke up with your high school sweetheart, or were fired from a job you loved. At the moment, it may have felt like you would never get over the sadness. But now, you can look back and realize that the situation was temporary, and you were stronger than you imagined. Time changed the way you feel. What lessons did you learn about yourself from those experiences? Can you take some of that new wisdom and apply it now in your time of greater emotional sadness?

Keep reminding yourself that even though you can't picture your future life being happy, you will learn to adjust to your new circumstances. Develop a mantra to repeat to yourself throughout the day. Something like, "I can do this." "I am strong. I can get through this." "It will be okay." "Breathe. Breathe. Breathe"

Having trustworthy and understanding friends will help you wade through the despair. You may have to reach out to them, as many times people don't know what to do or say, so they do or say nothing. It's not that they don't love or care about you. They just may need your cue that you need their company. Isolating yourself can pull you further into despair.

Be aware of your eating and sleeping habits. If they change drastically, this is a signal that you should reach out for help. Often people even think of suicide during the early months of grief. The pain and loneliness may seem overwhelming. It may feel like being with your loved one, wherever they are, would be better than trying to live through this on your own. If you have thoughts like this, you aren't crazy. But you do need help so that your thoughts don't turn to actual harm to yourself. If you were caught in a river's current, wouldn't you cry out for help? Never be embarrassed or ashamed to ask for a listening ear. Reach out to good friends who are willing to listen or, if necessary, find a professional coach, therapist or psychiatrist.

Your friends and family will probably be relieved to know that you want their assistance because they are also sharing your grief. They may even want to accompany you to a support group or a professional grief counselor.

BONUS MATERIAL:

Staying grounded: A trauma self-help exercise

It is very important to stay 'grounded.' If you are feeling disoriented, confused, or upset, you can do the following exercise:

- Sit on a chair. Feel your feet on the ground. Press on your thighs. Feel your behind on the seat and your back against the chair.
- Look around you and pick six objects that have red or blue. This should allow you to feel in the present, more grounded, and in your body. Notice how your breath gets deeper and calmer.
- You may want to go outdoors and find a peaceful place to sit on the grass. As you do, feel how your body can be held and supported by the ground.

Source: Gina Ross and Peter Levine, Emotional First Aid

DAILY READING

"Crisis can take you to the limits. Looking both ways-toward despair and hope, doubt and fear-you may be hard pressed to choose today. And the choice you make today will frequently change-tomorrow, if not before."
-David Biebel

Despair is the meeting of your deepest primal need for logic with a situation that makes no sense at all. It is physical aching. Every nerve ending is crying out, so you feel exhausted. Unable to understand what to do, your mind may ping-pong back and forth between thoughts of sadness and comfort, anger and guilt, things that need to be done and not caring.

Please be easy on yourself. The only thing you need to understand is that right now you need to live in the moment. Coach yourself into getting out of bed, taking care of your physical needs and reaching out for solace in the company of someone who can care for you.

Who can hold my hand through this day?

DAILY READING

**In times like these, it helps to recall that
there have always been times like these.**
–Paul Harvey

It may be hard to believe that anyone has felt the way you are feeling right now. Despair is "a loss of hope". The word *desperate* comes from despair. When you feel desperate, you can be frantic. Or you can feel like a wet mop in the corner of a public restroom-alone, forgotten, useless and sad. The rest of the world can be spinning in activity but you are mentally, emotionally and physically spent. The shock, hurt and anger have left you drained. This is the low point.

Others may try to cheer you up, but that just seems entirely pointless. Everything seems entirely pointless. You just want to stop feeling so completely sad. You may even wonder if you can go on; if life is worth living; if things will ever change and be better. Even though it seems impossible, your wondering is a good sign that your brain is trying to reason this out.

Before you give up, you must force your memory to search for times when you have been desperate before. They won't be comparable to this occurrence, but there have been instances where you were desperate to pass a test, get a job, be loved, get over an illness, or conquer a fear. These less momentous times were building blocks for now. Those small moments of triumph can be called upon as evidence that you have dealt with crisis before and moved through it.

What are some times when I felt desperation, but moved past it?

_____

_____

_____

_____

_____

_____

_____

_____

_____

_____

_____

_____

_____

_____

_____

_____

_____

_____

_____

_____

DAILY READING

> **I like living. I have sometimes been wildly, despairingly, acutely miserable, racked with sorrow, but through it all I still know quite certainty that just to be alive is a grand thing.**
>
> **–Agatha Christie**

It is good to remember the basics. Living is a good thing. It is the only thing we know. The alternative will come soon enough for us as well. It is also a good thing to remember that part of living is feeling all the range of emotions we have been blessed with.

Sorrow doesn't feel like a blessing. Grief doesn't seem to have any inherent benefit. Even animals have emotional grieving rituals. They seem to instinctively know that something sad and disturbing and final has happened.

In my opinion, deep grief is the path of resetting our minds to a new reality. Life will never be the same. There has to be a shift in energy that flows through our daily routine. Keeping in mind that living is a good thing, and that our loved one who is gone would want us to treasure every moment, will guide us through the dark days into a new reality of light and peace.

What are some of the things I can do today that remind me of how special it is to be alive?

_____

_____

_____

_____

_____

_____

_____

_____

_____

_____

_____

_____

_____

_____

_____

_____

_____

_____

_____

_____

DAILY READING

The bitterest tears shed over graves are for words left unsaid and deeds left undone.
-Harriott Beecher Stowe

Visiting the final resting place of your loved one is a very personal matter. Some are very comforted to be near them physically. Others find it too painful.

Every year, I take the two hour drive to visit my father's grave. He is laid to rest in the same cemetery as my grandparents, close to where I grew up. A few yards away is a beautiful regal gazebo, which always makes me smile. I spend time there in my solitary thoughts, and talk to him about what has happened in the last year. There are times that I sob at missing him, and there are times that I am peaceful. I am always grateful that during his long illness we were able to say what needed to be said before he died.

However, there will always be more to say. There will always be times in my life when I wish he was standing next to me. And those are where the tears come from.

If you want to visit the cemetery, do so. Perhaps at first a friend or family member can accompany you.

Take a few moments to have some private time to tell your loved one how much you miss them. None of us knows for certain what is heard, but I believe that sending your sentiments out into the universe they will be heard by someone who cares and understands, and that they will send back comfort and peace.

What do I wish I would have said or done?

_____

_____

_____

_____

_____

_____

_____

_____

_____

_____

_____

_____

_____

_____

_____

_____

_____

_____

DAILY READING

No matter how dark things seem to be or actually are, raise your sights and see the possibilities – always see them, for they're always there.

- *Norman Vincent Peale*

If you can't force yourself to see the possibilities that the future has to offer, you need to force yourself to confide in someone who can. There was a moment in my life when I said to my doctor, "I am going to walk into Camden tonight (the highest crime rated city in America) at 2am to get beat up, so that I look on the outside the way I am feeling on the inside." My guts were black and blue from desperation and sadness. But no one noticed. They would walk past me with smiles with no clue how distraught I was inside because I looked normal outside. Obviously, my depression had reached a dangerous low. My doctor immediately put me in a hospital for evaluation, therapy and treatment. It was the best seven days of my life because there I started to realize that I could begin to feel normal again. I saw others struggling, and that made me feel not so alone in my pain.

If you are dangerously low, and can't see your way out, go to your physician immediately. Call a suicide hotline, or a support group. Get online and find a support group that you can get an immediate response from. Stop a policeman, and tell them you need help. Drive to an emergency room and admit yourself.

Never be too embarrassed or ashamed to tell someone that you need help to be pulled from a dangerous depression. You may not be able to see the possibilities, but they are always there. When I think back to how I was feeling, and know now how my life has turned out, I am so glad I never turned my thoughts into action. I would have missed the best time of my life.

What level of despair am I feeling?

_____

_____

_____

_____

_____

_____

_____

_____

_____

_____

Can I see the possibilities that things will get better?

_____

_____

_____

_____

_____

_____

_____

_____

_____

_____

DAILY READING

Smooth seas do not make skillful sailors.
-African Proverb

If you have ever been in a boat in a storm, you know how alarming the feeling of being out of control can be. Skillful sailors learn how to behave in the face of storms. But until they live through one, they can't truly appreciate the strength that is required.

Life is never smooth sailing all the time. This current storm may have knocked the wind out of your sails. However, time does not stop moving forward. This storm will pass over, and calm will return. We all wish it could be different. Just keep remembering how strong you are. You can weather this storm, and you will be able to help someone else weather theirs.

Look around you to see who else is caught in the storm of despair. It may be the loved ones other family members, or even their pet. As in any emergency, when you help someone else it will help you by taking your mind off your hopelessness. Doing this will move you past gloom and begin to move you past the hardest part of the grieving process.

Who else is grieving that I can comfort?

_____

_____

_____

_____

_____

_____

_____

_____

_____

_____

What can we do to weather this storm together?

_____

_____

_____

_____

_____

_____

_____

_____

_____

_____

_____

Chapter 5

GRIEF – Anger comes from Hurt of Grief; Grief can lead to Despair; Despair can make us Angry

THE WEBSTER'S DICTIONARY defines "Grief" as "sadness, sorrow; a difficulty." The grief stage of loss sets in when despair starts to release its hold. You may feel like smiling would be inappropriate. During your day to day routine, others may observe you going about life, accomplishing your home or work duties, perhaps briefly smiling while acknowledging someone's presence. However, you are not smiling inside. This façade of normalcy is for the world to see. The sadness lying inside your soul is the grief that you are carrying with you at every moment. Being distracted by things to do, you may not be thinking about your lost loved one all the time, but dozens of times during the day, your sadness comes to the surface for moments, or minutes of time.

Everyone grieves differently, and for different lengths of time. You may know of someone who seemed to be able to return to life as usual shortly after the death of someone they loved. But remember, you are observing them from the outside. You aren't with them at every quiet moment of the day, or when they are alone at night. There is no "normal" period of grief.

Depending on your relationship with the one who has died, your grief will vary in length. The closer you were, the longer your grief may be prominent. Even after a few years, the longing to be with that person will always be there. Many spouses say they always miss their "other half". Parents who have lost children express never moving past their feelings of loss. They learn to live their lives in the absence of that loved one. But they hold them as a treasure in their hearts, and carry them forever in their souls.

My dad has been gone over twenty years. Very often I find myself thinking of him during a stressful day, when I'd like to pick up the phone and talk things over with him. Or when I hear an older man talk on and on while telling a story, I smile thinking about how I would roll my eyes and tell my dad "I don't have all day!" How I wish I could hear his voice now. I'd let him talk as long as he wishes, and I would cherish every wordy description. I'm not grieving him as I once did. But the thought of him both makes me happy, and sad. I'm sad because I miss his enormous hugs, and happy that we had such a wonderful time together. I hold our time together as precious. Looking back at his character, he taught me more about being a good, honest, hard working, charitable person then I ever realized. My life was better because he was in it, and still is.

The grief that you feel moves with you into the future because you are also grieving the loss of hopes, dreams and plans with that person. Perhaps you were planning a trip together, or wanted them to be a part of your future wedding, or be there at the birth of your child, or just had visions of growing old with them by your side. Now, planning the future is hard to imagine without them to share those moments. It is hard to imagine enjoying those same experiences alone. However, it is important to begin to plan something that you have always wanted to do in order to have something to look forward to. It seems impossible now, but it will be an incredible gift for yourself as time goes by.

For right now, remember that grief may manifest itself in physical feelings of headaches, tiredness, stomach problems, sleeplessness, aches and pains, panic attacks, even "seeing" the person. I remember once walking down a street and seeing my dead uncle walk past me. I quickly turned and ran up to him, only to find that the man was not my uncle. The man looked startled when I turned him around and said, "Uncle Tim?" "No," he replied, "I'm sorry." "I am too," I said feeling embarrassed and bewildered. Was my mind playing tricks on me? Was it Uncle Tim giving me a sign that he was okay? Since he had never had children, I was like a daughter to him. I was with him when he passed. He was a second dad to me after my father died, and losing him was like losing my father all over again. A lot of other people have told me they have had similar experiences of thinking they saw their lost loved ones. You may experience this too. It really helped to tell a friend my experience. It was kind of embarrassing admitting it, but when they assured me that they have heard it happening to others, or it happened to them, I felt like I wasn't crazy.

You may feel like just being alone, and refuse invitations to be with friends and family. Not wanting to be the "downer" at the gathering, or not wanting to see them having a good time and wondering how they could forget your loved one so easily could be reasons. If you need to be alone and cry away the evening with a sad movie, do it. But if you find you are isolating yourself after several months, grief counseling may be in order. If your grief has turned to depression, go to your doctor and discuss your feelings with him. Clinical depression can be treated briefly with antidepressants to stabilize your brain chemicals. Speaking with someone you trust, who either has been through a similar experience, or is trained to help those with depression caused by grief, will give you coping skills to move past the depression. Doing this is not being disloyal to your lost loved one. Nor is it showing that you have forgotten about them. It may be more comfortable for you to speak in a group of people who don't know you so that you don't feel judged or feel like you have to put up a front of being okay. Grief groups can be found at local churches, colleges and through your medical office.

So as you are wandering down the road with grief in your heart, please know that you are not alone. Your feelings and emotions of loss will come and go but will never be far away. As time passes and you move past the initial loss, your grief will become easier to bear. Memories of good times will replace memories of bad. Your heart will begin to feel less heavy. It is okay to move on with your life, enjoying times of laughter and fun with those you are sharing your life. Yes, your loved one would want you to remember them. But don't you think they would want you to also be happy?

<u>DAILY READING</u>

> **"Anyone can master a grief but he who has it."**
>
> *- **William Shakespeare***

People have no idea how to comfort you. Fact is, you have no idea how to be comforted. Even so, those around you will try to say wise things that will help you. They may seem nonchalant about giving advice, and walking away.

Remember Shakespeare's words. Then, remember that only you can truly understand your feelings. You will get past this moment. You, too, will return to "normal" living. But for right now, it is okay to just be.

It is normal to not care about the mundane things of life. Business may not seem like a priority. Cleaning your house could just seem totally unimportant. Staring at TV for hours helps to block out your thoughts and memories. Sleep provides comfort and peace. It's okay. You will be just fine.

What "should" I be doing right now that I don't feel like doing? Make a list. Do it later.

_____

_____

_____

_____

_____

_____

_____

_____

_____

_____

_____

_____

_____

_____

_____

_____

_____

_____

_____

_____

DAILY READING

The only courage that matters is the kind that gets you from one moment to the next.
- *Mignon McLaughlin*

Time is consistent no matter what is happening. A minute is always sixty seconds. An hour is always sixty minutes. However, when you are called upon to trudge through painful minutes, time may seem a lot slower. Linking those moments together requires courage.

Fortitude is something you may not think you possess. But those around you have seen how strong you have been at other times. Let them remind you of the trails and hardships that you have navigated before. Call on that bravery, boldness, and fearlessness NOW.

Ask someone to have coffee and allow them to comfort you with conversation and concern. If it is the middle of the night, call a friend. They will be glad they could do something to help you. Time will go faster when you are sharing it with someone who cares.

List times when you navigated through a difficult time and how you did it:

_____

_____

_____

_____

_____

_____

_____

_____

_____

_____

_____

_____

_____

_____

_____

_____

_____

_____

_____

_____

DAILY READING

> **Life does not cease to be funny when people die anymore than it ceases to be serious when people laugh.**
> **-Antoine de Saint – Exupery**

Someone said something funny. You hear yourself laugh out loud before you can stop yourself. Then you feel guilty. How can I be laughing at a time like this? What would my loved one think of me? What are others thinking of me? Do they think I have forgotten my grief? Do they think I don't love the one I lost?

Stop. Ask yourself how it felt to laugh. Disregard the internal critic, and focus on how you felt to let go and spontaneously laugh. Laughter is also a release of emotions. You don't have to stifle or monitor your reactions. If people judge you, shame on them. If you judge yourself, stop yourself mid-thought and give yourself permission to just be in the moment.

Repeat this to yourself: It's okay to feel good. My loved one would want me to enjoy every moment. It does not dishonor them in anyway.

DAILY READING

Sweet is a grief well ended.

-Aeschylus

Yes, grief does end. At least the initial painful grief of loss ends. It ends when you make the transition from focusing on their death, to focusing on their life. Remembering all the wonderful, beautiful, soulful qualities that enhanced your life will guide this shift from powerless mourning or powerful wisdom.

Sweet is knowing that you carry them with you. They are as close as closing your eyes and watching them laugh. Use their energy to forge your path to the future knowing that they will walk with you in anticipation for what will come next. They were meant to be in your life for a reason.

List all the important lessons you have learned just by knowing them.

_____

_____

_____

_____

_____

_____

DAILY READING

Death ends a life, not a relationship.
–Jack Lemmon

Relationship means "an emotional attachment". That attachment will always be in your heart and mind whether you are physically with the person or not.

You can maintain this relationship by thinking about them, talking to them, talking to others about them, and remembering all the wonderful times you had together. If you wished your relationship was a better one, you can analyze why it wasn't different so that you can use this knowledge to enhance your current relationships.

As your heart starts to release, you will begin moving past the first five stages of grief into the healing stages. One of them is finding lessons that will help you in the future. Start thinking about your current relationships.

Who do I want to be closer to? How can I make that happen?

_____

_____

_____

_____

_____

_____

_____

_____

_____

_____

_____

_____

_____

Part Two
Moving Past Starts Here

Chapter 6

SUPPORT – Seek friends, Counseling, Prayer

THE BEGINNING OF moving through your loss is reaching out for support. Some will have done this from the very beginning. Others will need to force themselves to stop the self-imposed isolation of grief and despair. When you feel like no one can truly understand the depth of your emotions, it is the normal reaction to keep to yourself, especially when well meaning friends and colleagues can say some pretty stupid and hurtful things without meaning to.

However, you need the support of others in everyday life to guide you through. This is easier if you have a well established spiritual family, such as a church or religious meeting place already. If you do not, or are not usually a religious person, you may hesitate to find spiritual help or counseling. The death of a loved one will bring up spiritual issues even if you are not a "believer". Often, those who are atheist or agnostic will have doubts and questions at this time about what they truly believe happens after death. Your mind may search for answers that will make sense and give you some comfort. It is hard to admit that your belief system may be in turmoil right now. It doesn't matter if you have strong faith in one particular belief, or no belief system at all. It is natural to find yourself wondering what really does happen after death.

You don't have to express these doubts to your friends or family. Just being with them will help you negate the isolation and give you things to do, places to go and other issues to think about so that you can move through your days with less focus on your confusion. Distraction is a good thing for your mind and soul. However, you should take some time to analyze your thoughts, feelings and beliefs in a renewed way now that you have this new experience to compare them to. Perhaps your beliefs have never been tested against actually losing someone you love. Perhaps now you are feeling differently, and can understand with more empathy and compassion how others have felt in the past when they went through this. Now may be the time you reach out to them as they will be able to understand the depths of your emotions, and you can ask them for how they handled moving past their loss.

Counseling should be considered if you have been grieving for a long time, and can't seem to move past the lack of energy and sadness. If your grieving is interfering in your normal activities for an extended period of time, a professional grief counselor will be able to help you work through why. Even in this 21st century, many people feel that it is shameful to go to a therapist. However, they wouldn't hesitate to go to a doctor for a physical ailment. Often, they will go and get an anti-depressant from their medical doctor. These medications, as discussed previously, are working to balance chemical reactions physically. A competent physician will recommend speaking with a psychiatrist or therapist along with these medications, as long term usage is not advised. Do not disregard this advice. Your whole being needs support at this time, not just the physical.

You may feel better speaking with a religious counselor such as a priest, minister or someone you know who is very spiritual and has experienced a loss. Choose someone who you feel comfortable with, someone trustworthy and empathetic. Remember that they are only human as well, and if they have lost someone close to them, they will be able to give you suggestions, pray with you, and comfort you. If the person you choose fails to help you, don't let that discourage you from trying again. Pray for direction. Heartfelt prayer helps you to lift the burden of grief and hand it over to your higher power. If you are angry at your higher power right now, that is also natural. So you ask, "How can I pray when I'm so angry at God?"

The Bible says to "pour out your heart". The book of Job contains hundreds of songs, prayers and conversations that Job had with God during his suffering and questioning of God's thoughts. When we are angry at someone, it doesn't help to ignore that person. The only way to move past the misunderstanding or miscommunication and heal our relationship is to speak with them. Sometimes we argue with them to get answers. God invites you to do the same with Him. Ask Him for support, for answers, for comfort. You can carry on a continuous conversation with God throughout the day. It doesn't have to be in a church or specific location. Whenever you need to speak with Him, do so. Even when friends or relatives are not available, He is. Even if you never prayed before, even if you didn't think you believed in God or that He can hear you, if you want to talk to God, do it. Humans have a spiritual side that can't be denied. Prayer will help build strength.

Another avenue of support is provided by Cindy Cipriani through Clear Path Institute, the provider of this book. She has been able to show people just like you how to move through this difficult time by using "The 5 C Solution", a unique formula that guides you when you need comfort, hope and direction. Cindy's contact information is on page 167. She would love to tell you more about her programs.

DAILY READING

When Christ said: "I was hungry and you fed me," he didn't mean only the hunger for bread and for food; he also meant the hunger to be loved. Jesus himself experienced this loneliness. He came amongst his own and his own received him not, and it hurt him then and it has kept on hurting him. The same hunger, the same loneliness, the same having no one to be accepted by and to be loved and wanted by. Every human being in that case resembles Christ in his loneliness; and that is the hardest part, that's real hunger.

- *Mother Teresa*

During your grief, you may never have felt so alone. Being without your loved one has left you feeling unloved. You are depleted emotionally, spiritually and physically.

Reach out to those around you who have been trying to help you. Allow their strength and love to envelope you. Feel their love. Even though you may still want to hide and be alone, push yourself to be cared for. You need to be loved right now.

DAILY READING

Shared joy is a double joy; shared sorrow is half a sorrow.

- Swedish Proverb

Don't you feel better when you talk about your problems to someone else? Haven't you ever been so upset that you couldn't see straight, but then you talk it over with a friend, and suddenly you find yourself smiling and understanding that it isn't so bad after all?

That is because you have just divided your burden in two. By allowing someone else to help you see past the emotions, you become lighter. Possibilities arise.

Who can I confide in to help carry my burden?

_____

Who has been there for me throughout this time?

_____

_____

_____

_____

_____

_____

_____

_____

_____

_____

_____

DAILY READING

> **'Tis not enough to help the feeble up, but to support them after.**
> **-William Shakespeare**

You are not an island. Your loss has affected others around you. As you grow in your strength day by day, they will also need support. Giving will feed you by helping you see that you are needed.

If you have lost a spouse, recognize that your children have lost a father or mother. If you have lost a child, recognize that your other children have lost a brother or sister.

They need you to not only recognize their grief but to also be there for them as they move through future joys and celebrations. They will always feel the loss as you will, but they also need you to pay attention to them outside of that shadow. This is never an easy balance. Continue to check with them to make sure their needs are being met.

Who needs my strength?

_____

_____

_____

_____

_____

How can I help them in their grief?

_____

_____

_____

_____

_____

_____

_____

_____

_____

_____

_____

_____

_____

_____

_____

_____

_____

_____

Chapter 7

ACTION – Take One Step Forward

"Ask Yourself: What is the ONE thing I can do to feel better in this moment?"

NEWTON'S LAW STATES, "The velocity of a body remains constant unless the body is acted upon by an external force." In other words, an object in motion stays in motion. Likewise, a body standing still, stays standing still until moved by an external force.

When your body is stuck in the emotional mud of grief, you will stay in the mud unless action is taken to get you out. The longer you are stuck, the more effort it will take to pull you out. Soon you and the mud become one and you are barely visible from each other.

The longer you have been unable to move through the death of a loved one, the harder the process will be to break the emotional and often physical bond you have formed with the sadness. The mud represents your belief system that is holding you.

You may believe that it is disloyal to move on. You may feel that people will think you didn't love the person you lost if you start living a "normal" daily routine. You may believe that being happy or smiling again shows a lack of respect. You may believe that if your loved one can see you, they would be hurt that you are living as though they had never died.

What are your beliefs that are holding you back from living life to its fullest right now? Ask yourself, Are my beliefs true? How would I want my loved ones to go on if I had been the one who died? Will people really judge me as unloving if I find joy? How would my loved one who is not here really want me to feel? Would they want me to grieve continuously?

The truth is that we all want our friends and family to love us and be sad that they no longer can be with us. But isn't it also true that we would only want them to mourn a little while, and then return to living without constant pain and grief? Everyone we love and lose becomes a piece of our hearts and memories that last our whole lives. We never truly move PAST loving them, we move past grieving them. Our grief can turn to happy thoughts and make us smile when they come to mind. We carry them with us every moment.

Challenging your emotional and mental mud will dilute it and make moving out of grief easier. Like adding water to mud, changing your thoughts will begin to dilute the guilt and let go of the sadness and pain. This mental exercise is the first step to Action.

Moving Past

Write down the challenges and new thoughts to begin to move past your tears.

_____

_____

_____

_____

_____

_____

_____

_____

_____

_____

_____

_____

_____

_____

_____

_____

_____

_____

Write down the activities you used to enjoy that you would like to enjoy again.

_____

_____

_____

_____

_____

_____

_____

_____

_____

_____

_____

_____

_____

_____

_____

_____

_____

Perhaps you need to find a new group of friends because it would be easier to be yourself around them. Often we think our friends and relatives expect us to still be mourning or expect that we would have moved past it. Our perception of their expectations can cause associating with our normal circle of friends and family awkward and difficult. Notice I said "our perception", because usually those who love us just want us to be happy. In these circumstances, they often really don't know what we need or how to help us. However, they also either don't want you to think they forgot, so they bring up the death and perhaps throw your mood back into grief; or they avoid the subject altogether, and you may find yourself annoyed because it seems they have gone on as if nothing has happened.

Either way, finding a group of people who have a common, positive interest as you do will help you be able to act as you want without analyzing how you are "supposed" to act.

Start a separate journal today. Think of one thing you can do to feel better <u>at this moment</u>, and write it down. Then force yourself to do it. Remember, your body, mind and emotion will want to stay exactly where they are. You must nudge yourself just one small step toward moving past your grief.

What is it that will make you feel better at this moment?

Stuck? How about calling a dear friend and asking them to meet you for coffee. Tell them that you are trying to move through your grief and need to talk about….whatever it is that is on your mind.

How about literally taking a walk? Your body is a machine. Physical activity of your body will stimulate your mind, get your blood flowing, send endorphins rushing through your veins, and give you energy to help move your mental state forward.

Force yourself to tune in to what you <u>really </u>need. If you feel like taking a drink, hitting something or doing anything self destructive, **don't**. Realize that those feelings are coming from anger. If that is how you are feeling, then what you really need is to go to Chapter Five. Your emotions are going to be all over the place right now. So follow them and try to root out the real cause. Close your eyes and really feel. Be true to what your gut needs. Find a positive step to take, and take it. It will take time to get easier, but it will. Once you are in motion, you will stay in motion. The pace may vary, but this is a marathon, not a sprint.

Marathon's are finished one step at a time. The runner's pace will vary during the race dependent on the terrain and their physical stamina. The body adjusts along the way to give more or less energy that is needed. Often runners will place people along the course at the mileage markers that they know are the hardest areas for them to mentally overcome. Some hit a wall around the 10 mile mark. So they will have someone there with water and to shout encouragement. Then again, around the 15 mile mark, or on an especially large hill someone will be in the middle cheering them on. The mind grabs this encouragement and computes that it can keep going despite the physical body being tired and worn. Your mind is a computer. You need to take action to help program it toward becoming strong and happy again with the help of those cheering you on.

Who can you count on to be there at your toughest times? Make a list, with their phone numbers and don't hesitate to call them. They will be glad you did. They want to help you.

For times when no one is available, like if night time is your hardest time because you are alone, make a play list of upbeat music to play. Music that makes you smile! Play it as loud as you like (or wear a headset if it will disturb your neighbors) and dance! It will fill your mind with positive thoughts during your sleep and the dancing will help make your body tired enough to rest.

Your body in motion will pull itself out of the mud of grief little by little with consistent and supported effort. Try it.

What is the one thing I can do right now to feel better?

_____

_____

_____

_____

_____

_____

_____

Make this question your mantra. Soon it will be a habit. Then it will become natural to feel alive again without the guilt.

DAILY READING

Follow effective action with quiet reflection. From the quiet reflection will come even more effective action.

-Peter Drucker

Quiet reflection will help align your thoughts with appropriate action. Often your life seems to be at warp speed as the days fly by. But at times of loss, the days slow down. This stillness provides an opportunity to re-evaluate your goals, priorities, and future plans. Adjustments need to be made now that your situation is different. How to begin?

Choose a quiet place where you can feel peaceful. Listen to your thoughts. Get in touch with your feelings. Jot down the questions you have. Note your physical responses to your thought patterns. Play soulful music. Pray. Ask for guidance.

DAILY READING

Pleasure and action make the hours seem short.

-William Shakespeare

Did you ever notice how time seems to go by faster when you are engaged in an activity that you enjoy? Give yourself permission to seek pleasurable activities and do things that make your day go faster. Time has slowed down in your grief, and now needs to be brought back to normal. Giving yourself permission is essential to this balance. It may feel reproachable to be enjoying yourself in light of your loss. It is not. Life is made for joy.

What activities can I do that will make the hours fly by?

_____

_____

_____

_____

_____

_____

_____

What pleasures can give pardon to my pain?

_____

_____

_____

_____

_____

_____

_____

_____

_____

_____

_____

_____

_____

_____

_____

_____

_____

_____

DAILY READING

Action is a great restorer and builder of confidence. Inaction is not only the result, but the cause, of fear. Perhaps the action you take will be successful; perhaps different action or adjustments will have to follow. But any action is better than no action at all.

-*Norman Vincent Peale*

Moving forward takes effort. But nothing will get accomplished unless you take action. Your life path will curve and weave. There is never a straight path to happiness, success or accomplishment. There are ups and downs, trials and tribulations, joy and sorrow. But if you don't try, nothing will happen.

How do you want to feel?

Fearful or Confident? Successful or Defeated?

The only difference is the amount of effort and persistence that you put forth.

What action can I take to move forward?

_____

_____

_____

_____

_____

_____

_____

_____

_____

_____

_____

_____

_____

_____

_____

_____

_____

_____

_____

_____

DAILY READING

> **Repetition of the same thought or physical action develops into a habit which, repeated frequently enough, becomes an automatic reflex.**
>
> ***-Norman Vincent Peale***

Today pay attention to your thoughts. Write them down. Are you repeating the same thoughts over and over? Are they negative or positive? Habits are hard to break. But not impossible. If it has become a habit to be sad and hopeless, it will take concentration on your thoughts to move past the darkness of negativity into the light of day.

What habits do I have that I need to change to be happy?

_____

_____

_____

_____

_____

_____

_____

_____

_____

_____

_____

_____

_____

_____

_____

_____

_____

_____

_____

DAILY READING

> **Forgiveness is the key to action and freedom.**
> **-Hannah Arendt**

Being stuck is sometimes the result of guilt. Do you feel guilty that you are alive and able to go on with your life when your loved one can't? Do you re-run the last argument you had with them over and over in your mind, feeling guilty because of the things you said? Do you regret not taking more time from your schedule to spend with them while you had the opportunity?

Forgiving yourself is the key to freedom from guilt and grief.

What do I need to forgive myself for? _____

_____

_____

_____

_____

How? Stand in front of a mirror and tell yourself that you are forgiven for whatever has been gnawing at you. Take deep breathes until you are relaxed, and then tell yourself again. Be a friend to yourself, and accept the forgiveness. Feel the guilt leave your body. Breathe again and smile at yourself.

Give yourself a huge hug. Now go about your day.

What are my habitual thoughts?

_____
_____
_____
_____
_____
_____
_____
_____
_____
_____
_____
_____
_____
_____
_____
_____
_____
_____
_____
_____

DAILY READING

> **All action results from thought, so it is thoughts that matter.**
>
> **-Sai Baba**

Now that you know the thoughts that are blocking you from fully living life, you need to focus on challenging them. The negative record in your head can be disconnected by purposely stopping the track when it starts to play. When you are conscious of your thoughts, you can stop them midstream and ask yourself,

"Is that thought true? Is that how I want to be thinking?"

Then, change the thought to direct you toward the positive. If you need to literally stop whatever you are doing at the time, then stop. Focus and force yourself to redirect your thought pattern.

It is worth paying close attention to your thoughts! It will change your life.

Thought: _____

_____

_____

_____

Is that true?

_____

_____

_____

_____

_____

_____

Focus on Reality and Think This:

_____

_____

_____

_____

_____

_____

_____

_____

_____

_____

_____

_____

_____

_____

_____

_____

_____

_____

_____

_____

DAILY READING

**When thought becomes excessively painful,
action is the finest remedy.**

–Salman Rushdie

When Cesar Milan, the Dog Whisperer, rehabilitates the bad behavior of a dog, he simply redirects their thought at the moment of the behavior by tapping them or making a sudden sound to distract them. You can do the same thing when your thoughts are bringing you pain.

Suddenly getting up and walking around, changing the subject when speaking to someone who is upsetting you, or putting on fun music can remedy the negative thoughts.

Write down some strategies that will help redirect you out of negative thoughts:

_____

_____

_____

_____

_____

_____

_____

_____

_____

_____

_____

_____

_____

_____

_____

_____

_____

_____

_____

DAILY READING

The best thing about giving of ourselves is that what we get is always better than what we give. The reaction is greater than the action.
-Orison Swett Marden

When you focus on what you don't have instead of what you do, it is easy to get down. Today take notice of all the wonders in your life. What are all the things you have that add joy? Remembering that there are so many people who don't have the basic necessities of life, can help you appreciate how blessed you truly are. Why not get out of your own circumstances and volunteer at a shelter, food bank, charity or organization to help others. You will achieve a new sense of value, self-esteem and humility.

Look up local volunteer opportunities and sign up this week. Don't just look on the internet and then forget about it. Actually GO and help.

What organization(s) can I help?

_____

_____

_____

_____

_____

_____

_____

_____

_____

When am I going to volunteer?

_____

_____

_____

_____

_____

_____

_____

_____

_____

_____

_____

_____

_____

_____

_____

_____

_____

_____

_____

DAILY READING

There is nothing terribly wrong with feeling lost, so long as that feeling precedes some plan on your part to actually do something about it. Too often a person grows complacent with their disillusionment, perpetually wearing their "discomfort" like a favorite shirt.
- Jhonen Vasquez

Your life path has taken a detour. Will you sit at the crossroad motionless? Will you dart off in some unknown direction? Will you tell every passerby that you are lost, with no intention of taking their help?

Or will you examine your choices, consult your internal GPS and move in the direction of your life's purpose? We are planners by nature. Having a plan, although different than what you may have planned before, is the way to move past the feeling of loss. Give yourself permission to move ahead. "Recalculate" your position, and move forward.

What is my GPS (Grief Permission Status)?

_____

_____

_____

_____

_____

What is my internal guidance system telling me to do?

_____
_____
_____
_____
_____
_____
_____
_____
_____
_____
_____
_____
_____
_____
_____
_____
_____
_____
_____
_____

DAILY READING

> *He who is outside his door has the hardest*
> *part of his journey behind him.*
> ### - Flemish Proverb

Being a jogger, I think of this saying every morning as I get out of bed. There are times when I can't wait to put on my sneakers and fly down the road. But most of the time, getting out the door is the most difficult part of my run.

There are so many distractions. The morning news, e-mail to check, laundry to fold, work to organize, appointments to keep, etc. Even though I know my thighs will not get any smaller if I miss my run, there are days where the minutes disappear leaving me no time for my jog. Then all day, I beat myself up because I missed the exercise I know I need.

In the guilt, I end up eating a chocolate cupcake to feel better, and before you know it, I'm depressed. Yes, just getting out the door could alleviate so much!

What door is your hardest obstacle?

_____

_____

_____

_____

_____

_____

_____

_____

_____

_____

_____

_____

_____

_____

_____

_____

_____

_____

_____

DAILY READING

Like a welcome summer rain, humor may suddenly cleanse and cool the earth, the air and you.

-Langston Hughes,
The Book of Negro Humor

Laughter may seem out of place in your life right now. However, it may be just the medicine you need to cleanse your soul. Think about your loved one for a minute. When their face comes to mind, were they smiling? A smile is a gift to everyone around you. Don't hold back that gift from those who love you. Leave your smile as a photo in their minds. You may not be ready for a comedy club, but enjoying others humor will decrease your stress and the stress of those you love.

Why do you feel guilty about laughing?

Why do you think you feel any less loss if you smile?

Are you holding on to sadness as a way of holding on to your loved one?

What is a better way to honor them?

Chapter 8

STRENGTH – continued action

THERE IS NOTHING that can bring you to your knees like losing someone you love. No matter how strong you are physically, the mourning period can make you feel weak. As previously discussed, some of this comes from our literal body trying to deal with the stress, lack of sleep, and not eating properly. Some of the weakness is due to your emotional turmoil. But after you start taking action, one step at a time, toward your normal routine, strength will return.

If you have ever tried to get in shape by lifting weights, you realize that strength training does not come overnight. Sure the first day you feel like you could work out forever! You look around the gym and think, "Wow, this isn't so hard! I'll look like a bodybuilder in no time!"

But the next day, you can hardly get out of bed. Every muscle hurts. Now it takes mental strength to go back to the gym. You have to really talk yourself into it, because now your body knows that it is hard work and it will take time. Perseverance is the key.

The same thing applies when you are trying anything new. I have always admired people who play musical instruments because for years I tried to play the piano with no success. I know how much time and practice it takes to play beautifully.

Moving past this awful time of your life will take time and perseverance also. You will go through all the emotions in your own order and time period. As you go on this journey, there are things you can do to start building strength to go on.

As with lifting weights, start light. Doing the exercises at the bottom of each daily reading will allow you to develop the habit of journaling your thoughts, emotions and feelings. Writing provides an outlet and a history of your progress. It may seem strange at first, but if you stick with it, you will find that recording your feelings at the end of the day before you go to sleep will become something that you look forward to as a way to dump everything onto paper and release yourself from anxiety and stress so you can sleep.

> An excerpt from Cindy's journal six months after Rosie's death:
>
> It's 3am. I can't sleep. I miss Rosie. I should have spent more time with her. Why was I always so busy? I bet she thought I didn't care. I was so selfish. How I would love to call her up and go have lunch. I miss her laugh. I miss how she made me laugh. I hope she is in heaven dancing with her husband. That would be nice. Tomorrow I have to get up early. Work is piling up. Rosie-wherever you are I hope you know I love you. Good night.

After a few months, you can go back and read what you have written to see if and how your feelings have changed. Using this as a measurement, you will know what kind of help or assistance you may need to continue to get stronger and return to living with less pain.

During times of grief your thinking can become distorted. You could start thinking in language that is black and white; all or nothing, generalizing the grief you are feeling so that it seems to cover all areas of life. Take a look at what you are saying to yourself and see if you notice any of these thoughts. Ask yourself the question, "Is what I am thinking really true?"

112

In the previous Journal Entry, notice how Cindy was using "Should" statements, Labeling and Blaming. Asking "Is it true?" would enable her to see that she spent a lot of time with Rosie; Rosie didn't think she didn't love her; and even though she wished they had more time together, the times they had were wonderful.

Think of your loved one and the good times you had together. Remember how they added joy to your life.

Stepping back from your inner thoughts and analyzing the facts can pull you from falling backward into the hurt and anger phases. For example, if you start thinking, "Life sucks."

Ask yourself, "Is it true?" Make a list of all the things in the past day or two that have happened that you enjoyed. Perhaps indulging in your favorite dessert, having lunch with a friend, smelling a rose…anything that brought you joy. Or, if you think, "I will never be happy again." Ask yourself, "Is it true?" Think back to other times when you thought the same thing and recovered. This may seem silly, but it really works. It's called a mental shift. You can make 'mind over matter' work if you can step out of the emotions for a few minutes and concentrate on logic. Think like Spock from Star Trek. Again, seems silly, but it works.

Another strategy is to start doing something you like to do. Perhaps you want to join a bowling league, start rollerblading in the park, do quilting with a club, go out dancing with a few friends, dig into landscaping your back yard, etc. All of these actions will begin to move you past your grief by pulling yourself out of the mental focus on the pain. As time goes by, you will be concentrating on positive, even fun, activities, instead of being pulled back into the sadness of loss. You will always feel the emptiness of not having your loved one with you. But over time, you will begin to move past not being able to move, and begin to again enjoy activities.

Another tactic to use is music. While I have no musical ability, I am totally grateful for the writers and musicians that fill our lives with songs. Music is a powerful implement that moves us. Did you ever notice how you could be having a good day, and then you hear a song on the radio that makes you cry? It can also work the opposite way.

On a day when you are having a hard time crawling out of bed, turn on an upbeat dance tune, and soon you will find your feet tapping. Well, maybe not tapping, but at least you will have the will to get out from under the sheets. So why not use this to help you? Go to iTunes and make a "pick me up" song list of your favorite songs. Actually, make several for each mood you may be in, or may want to get out of. Make a list of sad songs to help you cry when you need to. Make a list of angry songs when you feel like no one understands you. Make a list of "Okay I have pitied myself long enough songs". And make one of happy dance tunes that will pull you up from the pits of depression. Keep them handy for times when you are quiet or alone. Play them in your car (well, not the angry one). Play them at home. Play them when you are exercising, which is also a great way to burn off emotions and get stronger physically at the same time.

As time moves past, strength will help you take the action you need to recover. Be patient with yourself. Strength takes time. The key is to keep moving. Be easy on yourself, but not too easy. Pushing past the pain will lead you to enjoying life again. Continued Action = Strength.

DAILY HELPER:

Starting a <u>"To Do" Journal</u> is a wonderful tool to help you feel like you are accomplishing tasks and provides a log of activity as evidence of your progress.

Every night before you go to sleep, write down four things to do the next day.

They should include:

1. Physical Activity – Exercise will release endorphins to elevate your mood.
2. Spiritual – Do something that eases your spirit. For example: Volunteer, Pray, Help Someone, Read an uplifting book, etc.
3. Mental – Get the everyday tasks done to release your mind of stress and worry
4. Fun – Do something you really enjoy. For example: Eat your favorite dessert, watch your favorite TV show, Meet a friend for coffee, etc.

DAILY READING

Music was my refuge. I could crawl into the spaces between the notes and curl my back to loneliness.

- Maya Angelou

If only life had background music! In the movies, just as the heroine is about to show some great act of strength or courage, the orchestra swells in melodious accompaniment. We sit at the edge of our seats, willing her on as the music resonates in our souls. Somehow the music seems to propel her beyond normal to become victorious against insurmountable odds.

Music has a direct connection to our emotions. We can use it to energize us in the morning, calm us at night, purge our soul, entice memories, bring solace and peace. Certain songs can connect us to our lost loved ones.

Today create your own background music. Choose songs that will give you strength and move you through the day.

Create your own iTunes list for different moods.

DAILY READING

Strength does not come from physical capacity. It comes from an indomitable will.
-Mohandas Gandhi

Even the strongest man in the world will lose his strength if he stops lifting weights. His true strength is the will to get out of bed every morning and continue the routine of exercise necessary to maintain or increase his muscle mass.

"Indomitable" means "determined, impossible to defeat." You have this will inside you. Call it out today. Be determined to move forward and not allow this loss to overwhelm you.

What routine can I establish that will continue to make me strong?

_____

_____

_____

_____

_____

_____

_____

_____

_____

_____

_____

_____

_____

_____

_____

DAILY READING

The difference between a successful person and others is not a lack of strength, not a lack of knowledge, but rather a lack of will.
-Vince Lombardi

Will power can propel us to achieve more than others think is possible. Lack of will power will keep us entrenched and stuck. It is hard to have the will to go forward when we have been kicked in the gut, with all our air sucked out of us.

Vince Lombardi knew about perseverance. As the head coach of the Green Bay Packers during the 1960's, he led the team to four straight league championships, including winning the first two Super Bowls. He never had a losing season as head coach in the NFL. What made him different than the other coaches? A relentless pursuit of victory.

Our team in life, our friends, family and associates, can help infuse strength to us when we need it. Choose one special person that can be your strength coach to see you through this time, be at your side, and encourage your will.

I choose _____ to be my coach.

DAILY READING

Anxiety does not empty tomorrow of its sorrows, but only empties today of its strength.

-Charles Spurgeon

Worry and anxiety are meditation on the negative. These thoughts can cloud your mind and rob you of happiness. You can't change the past. You can't guarantee what will happen in the future. You just have today. One moment at a time.

Establishing a routine will help you regain your strength. Write three things to do the moment you open your eyes in the morning that will return you to a routine. Example:

1. Say thanks for another day.
2. Stretch
3. Make coffee.

Three Things I can do the moment I open my eyes tomorrow:
1. _____
2. _____
3. _____

DAILY READING

**Women are like teabags. We don't know
our true strength until we are in hot water!**
-Eleanor Roosevelt

No one likes to think of life as a test of strength, but often it is. When you look back over your life, think of the times when you thought things couldn't get any worse. Times when you thought you would never be happy again. It took time, but those times past and you were happy again. In fact, you can probably think of a lesson or two that you learned from going through that stressful time. Your endurance muscles were being strengthened. You were able to use solutions and strategies that stretched your survival abilities.

When you are feeling drained, pour yourself a cup of boiling water, seep a teabag in it, and remember how strong you really are. Sweeten and add lemon. Then sit and relax.

Repeat to yourself out loud, "I am strong. I am strong. I am strong." Feel the warmth as you swallow and allow the hug of comfort to embrace you.

DAILY READING

It does not take much strength to do things, but it requires great strength to decide on what to do.

-Elbert Hubbard

Mind over matter, right? Deciding how to get through the day can be the hardest thing you do all day. It can feel easy to bury your head under the covers and vegetate. But before long your physical body will need to eat, drink, go to the bathroom, all requiring that you move even though you don't want to. The moral of this is that at times, you need to just listen to your body to decide how to move through the day.

What does your body need today? Nourishment? Exercise? Rest? Laughter? A massage? To lay in the sun? Hone in on exactly what your body is asking for. Decide to give it what it needs. Feel stronger for taking care of yourself.

Today I need: _____

DAILY READING

You gain strength, courage, and confidence by every experience in which you really stop to look fear in the face. You are able to say to yourself, 'I lived through this horror. I can take the next thing that comes along.'
-*Eleanor Roosevelt*

On September 11, 2001, 2,819 people lost their lives. The lives of their families, friends, co-workers and fellow Americans were changed in an instant. This was the largest horror to ever occur on American soil. The grief is still culpable a decade later.

The wives, husbands and children of those lost realize that they lived through this unspeakable horror as a collective group. However, each individual carries their grief in a unique and personal way. The strength that they have gained has made them who they are today, and capable of handling anything. It has made them empathetic to others suffering and appreciative of the shortness of life. Their courage is a model for anyone grieving. Think of all the children whose lives were changed to give you strength on your journey. They miss their parents every moment, but have learned to live with them missing the wonderful events of their lives. Many say they are stronger and live with happiness in honor of the parent they no longer can kiss goodnight. If they can do it, so can you.

Ask: Who do I know that serves as an example of survival? How can they inspire me?

_____

_____

_____

_____

_____

_____

_____

_____

_____

_____

_____

_____

_____

_____

_____

_____

_____

_____

_____

_____

_____

DAILY READING

Where there is no struggle, there is no strength.

-Oprah Winfrey

If we could avoid struggle and pain, we would. But it is the struggles and pain that makes us stronger. Mentally, physically and emotionally we can find out that we have strength beyond what we thought possible. Our thoughts bring reality. Concentrate today on bringing strength into your life. Close your eyes, breathe deeply and allow the energy of the universe to penetrate your body filling you with courage, determination and power to move forward.

Focus on all the wonderful people in your life; all the delicious tastes of the food you eat; the smell of flowers; the heat of the sun on your face; the warmth of your home. Show nothing but appreciation for all you have today. Joy is in the details.

What is wonderful in my life right now?

_____
_____
_____
_____
_____
_____
_____

Why?

_____
_____
_____
_____
_____
_____
_____
_____
_____
_____
_____
_____
_____
_____
_____
_____
_____

DAILY READING

**Good actions give strength to ourselves
and inspire good actions in others.**

-Plato

Sometimes when you are caught up in the overwhelming sadness of grief, you miss the actions of others who are trying to help. You can feel alone while there is a whole network of those who love you reaching out. Their good actions (bringing you food, calling, stopping by, sending cards, doing errands) can go unnoticed at first. But as you get stronger, think about those who were there. Reach out to them with thanks and appreciation.

Your thanks will inspire them to continue to reach out to help others in their time of need. Write thank you cards, call them and personally tell them that the things they did for you made a difference. Give them a hug. Use their positive energy and go out and help someone else today.

Who do I need to thank?

_____

_____

_____

_____

_____

_____

_____

_____

_____

_____

_____

_____

_____

_____

_____

_____

_____

_____

DAILY READING

Unity is strength . . . when there is teamwork and collaboration, wonderful things can be achieved.

-Mattie Stepanek

Mattie's observation reminded me of Matthew 18:20 that states, "Where there are two or three gathered together in my name, there I am in their midst." Both are referring to the presence of spirit that occurs in a group of people with a joint agenda. Why is that?

It is like adding logs to a fire. The more you add, the larger the bonfire becomes. The bigger the source of energy and warmth. Part of gaining your strength back will come from gathering with your friends and family. Joining a group where you have a common interest, like a hobby or sport, will bring the same strength to you. Fight the feeling of wanting to be alone. Pray to be guided to a group that will assist in healing you, and distract you. You need to laugh. You need to live fully.

Who can I use as my team?

_____
_____
_____
_____
_____
_____
_____
_____
_____
_____
_____
_____
_____
_____
_____
_____
_____
_____
_____

DAILY READING

You have power over your mind - not outside events. Realize this, and you will find strength.

-Marcus Aurelius

We create our own reality. That statement may make you angry if you have just lost someone because you would never have wanted your reality to include this loss.

Even though you can't change circumstances, only you can control your reaction to it. How your mind processes the loss will affect how much strength you have going forward.

Be aware of your thoughts. Challenge them. Don't let your emotions control your thoughts, but fight to have your thoughts control your emotions. You have the power over your mind. Program your mind to do good in honor of your loved one and you will find strength.

Ways I can honor my loved one:

_____
_____
_____
_____
_____
_____
_____
_____
_____
_____
_____
_____
_____
_____
_____
_____
_____
_____
_____

DAILY READING

> **Only by contending with challenges that seem to be beyond your strength to handle at the moment you can grow more surely toward the stars.**
>
> *-Brian Tracy*

No you didn't want this challenge. You would do anything not to have to go through this. At times it seems that you can't bare it. Remind yourself that you are stronger than you know. You don't have to take this journey alone. Reach out to your cheerleaders for help when the journey becomes too difficult to manage alone. Even months or years later, you may find yourself having a difficult day or two. It's okay to let someone know. Sharing the burden by borrowing someone else's strength will allow you to keep going.

Write down challenges that you have overcome in the past as a reminder of how strong you are:

_____

_____

_____

_____

_____

_____

_____

_____

_____

_____

_____

_____

_____

_____

_____

_____

_____

_____

_____

Chapter 9

MEMORY TREASURE CHEST –
Store positive memories

A S TIME GOES by, when you think of your loved one, more and more good memories will come to mind. If they had been ill or suffered for a time, you may think that you will always remember them in that sickly condition.

When my father was suffering from lung cancer, he transformed from a strong, muscular, hard working 59 year old, to a weak, emaciated, bedridden 62 year old who looked more like 92. It was heart wrenching to watch. Before he died, he asked that a viewing not be arranged for his funeral. He said it was because "anyone who truly cared about me would have already seen me before I died." However, I believe it also had to do with him not wanting everyone to see him at his final state. It was hard enough watching the transformation day by day. For anyone who hadn't seen him during the illness, they would have been shocked.

Despite his wishes, my mother decided to have a viewing, leaving my father in the very capable hands of his friend who was also the mortician. I was appalled at this decision. But when I went to see him before it started, I was amazed to see that he had been restored to his pre-illness handsomeness. Perhaps it helped that the mortician was his friend, and knew him for many years when he was well. But for whatever reason, I was glad that I was able to see him looking like himself one last time.

I thought that I would never get those last few months out of my mind, but slowly my memories were of him when he was at his best. Now when I think of my dad, I think of his laugh, the way he would take half an hour giving directions which included every detail along the way (*i.e. you go down the road a bit until you see the big walnut tree in the fork in the road…that tree was planted there when I was a boy…I remember because that is the way we used to go…anyway, you turn right at the fork and….*), and the scratch of his whiskers on my cheek when he hugged me. As the years have gone by, I have more and more wonderful memories, and rarely think of the suffering except to remember how brave, strong and determined he was.

Literal Memory Treasure Chests are a fantastic way to keep your happy memories at the forefront as you move ahead in time. Choose a special box and store photographs, clippings, special items in it that will make you smile whenever you open it. Perhaps saving their cologne or a favorite item can be included.

Write down your memories of special times you had with them or any special advice that they gave you. Video tapes may be hard to look at right now, but years from now it may just what you need to remember their voice, laughter and gestures.

The first time I watched my family reunion video which contained my dad telling a joke to the camera and then snorting as he laughed at himself, I cried. But they were happy tears because I was so happy to see him and hear his voice again after such a long time. Each time I watch it, it becomes easier and is like a short visit with him that always makes me laugh. Being able to share that video with my children is a special treat, as they were very young when he passed away and they really don't remember him at his prime.

Probably one of the hardest tasks you will be faced with if you have lost a spouse or child, is deciding what to do with their possessions. Everyone has so much "stuff". When you start to sort through it, memories will pour forth. Realize that those memories will not leave you even if the literal object does. Some people want to leave everything exactly as the person left it. Perhaps even years later, their bedroom or office is untouched. While others, clear everything out too soon because they can't bear to see all the reminders.

TIPS:

1. Don't try to do this alone. Call a friend or relative who has more perspective at this highly emotional time to help you sort through possessions.

2. Create a Memory Treasure Chest and add to it whenever you come across a special item or photograph.

3. Listen to your own pace. If you need time, take the time.

4. Don't make any major decisions, like selling the house and moving, for at least a year. Your needs, thoughts and wants will change and even though it may be hard to be around all the memories at first, they may become a comfort after some time.

5. Secure professional help from accountants, lawyers, and insurance agents if you are in charge of an estate. These experts will have the clear heads to guide you through the process of paperwork, finances and legal necessities.

DAILY READING

> **Happiness is good health and a bad memory.**
>
> **- *Ingrid Bergman***

Oh if only we could take the difficult memories and forget them. Perhaps we could be more childlike. Children have great stamina but short memories. They cry one minute and laugh the next. They don't hold grudges. They make sure everyone knows when they are hungry, tired, or need to be changed. They don't mind depending on others to carry them. When they are bored, they run away and find something fascinating to do. They have endless energy. Learning something new is thrilling. Sleep is sound and peaceful. Their smiles are contagious.

How can I be more childlike today?

_____

_____

_____

_____

_____

_____

_____

_____

_____

_____

_____

_____

_____

_____

_____

_____

_____

_____

_____

DAILY READING

The best portion of a good man's life is his little, nameless, unremembered acts of kindness and of love.
- *William Wordsworth*

Were you surprised at some of the stories people told you about your loved one after they died? Each person who knew them had a different experience that endeared them. Often it is the small acts of kindness that they did without even thinking that made a huge difference in the lives of others.

Write some of these little acts of kindness and love down.

Keep them in your memory chest to reflect on. Perhaps you could imitate some of their deeds in honor of them.

_____

_____

_____

_____

_____

_____

_____

_____

_____

_____

_____

_____

_____

_____

_____

DAILY READING

No memory is ever alone; it's at the end of a trail of memories, a dozen trails that each have their own associations.
-Louis L'Amour, Ride the River

When someone leaves this life, we have a tendency to remember every detail about their passing. We know exactly where we were when we heard the news. We relive the last conversation we had with them. We can picture the moments over and over. This is normal because our minds are trying to reconcile something which is irreconcilable. We tell the story over and over to all that will listen.

But as time goes on, our memory will expand to all the connected memories of our past with them. Over time, you will be able to think past the moment of their passing and focus on all the precious life experiences you shared.

Allow your mind to drift down the trail of memories.

DAILY READING

At the end of the games, the king and the pawn go back in the same box.
– *Italian Proverb*

It is often said that life is a game. One thing is true-every game has a beginning and an end. There are winners and losers. The learning comes from the strategy. Everyone has a life of good moves and bad ones. No matter how much money you have accumulated, what type of car you drive, how big your house is, or how famous you are, nothing can stop you from someday ending the game of life.

This is a good time to reflect, and make all the right moves so that no matter when your game is over, you will feel like a winner.

So how do I want to play the game of life? What *really* matters to me?

_____

_____

_____

_____

_____

_____

_____

_____

_____

_____

_____

_____

_____

_____

_____

_____

_____

_____

_____

_____

DAILY READING

**Keep some souvenirs of your past, or how
will you ever prove it wasn't all a dream?
- *Ashleigh Brilliant***

Why do people buy souvenirs when they travel? Because years later they can hold them and their mind transports them back to the very moment when they got them. Souvenirs of your loved one may hurt to hold on to at first. But don't give everything away. The day will come when you will need to be transported back to the past to be with them again.

Holding my dad's reading glasses takes me back to his side in my parent's kitchen where he would sit and read the paper in his flannel shirt and work pants. I can smell the coffee in the mug that he holds. And as my eyes fill with tears at this memory, I smile and remember how healthy and strong he looks. It wasn't a dream. I had a wonderful father who wore cheap brown drugstore reading glasses and looked like a million bucks in them.

What are your favorite souvenirs that bring your loved one back to life in your memory?

_____

_____

_____

_____

_____

_____

_____

_____

_____

_____

_____

_____

_____

_____

_____

_____

_____

_____

_____

DAILY READING

**Recollection is the only paradise from
which we cannot be turned out.**
– Jean Paul Righter

Palm trees, blue water, sand and surf. These are no doubt mental images you conjure up when thinking of paradise.

The emotional side of paradise is calm, peaceful and relaxing. Try to attach these feelings with the picture of your loved one's face. Close your eyes and see them laughing. Think of a time when you were enjoying each other's company. Even in tumultuous relationships, there were times of joy.

When you make this connection, reflecting on the memories will be a wonderful experience. Try it. Practice it. Especially on difficult days, retreat to paradise. Sit outside, put an umbrella in your drink and put your feet up. Pretend they are enjoying this moment with you. Ah, paradise.

Chapter 10

RECORD A LESSON – Physically write down what you have learned from this experience

EVERYTHING THAT HAPPENS to you teaches you a lesson. Losing someone you love is not the kind of lesson you want to experience. However, since it has happened, after time has passed and you have moved past the initial time of grief, it is a good time to reflect on what you have learned by going through this experience. Has your level of empathy grown for others experiencing a similar loss? Have you become more in touch with your spiritual emotions? Has your belief system been changed?

It is my belief that every time we experience heartache, we develop an emotional scar. Our hearts were ripped open and had to go through the healing process. Slowly, the wound was filled in, and a file of that experience was put into our memory banks. Before you tuck it away and go about leading your life, record what lessons you have learned so that you can pull out the final outcome and remember that you will be able to navigate grief if you ever lose anyone else in the future.

WHAT I HAVE LEARNED ABOUT LOSS:

_____

_____

_____

_____

_____

_____

_____

_____

_____

WHAT I HAVE LEARNED ABOUT MYSELF:

_____

_____

_____

_____

_____

_____

_____

_____

_____

WHO I CAN COUNT ON TO BE THERE FOR ME:

_____

_____

_____

_____

_____

_____

_____

_____

_____

_____

WHAT HELPED ME MOVE PAST LOSS THE MOST:

_____

_____

_____

_____

_____

_____

_____

_____

_____

_____

WHAT HELPED ME MOVE PAST THE LEAST:

_____

_____

_____

_____

_____

_____

_____

_____

_____

WHAT I HAVE LEARNED ABOUT THE PROCESS:

_____

_____

_____

_____

_____

_____

_____

_____

_____

_____

DAILY READING

Pray that your loneliness may spur you into finding something to live for, great enough to die for.
- Dag Hammarskjold

Feeling desperate to regain the relationship you shared with your loved one is a loneliness like no other. You may be surrounded by other people, but feel alone in your unique grief. One way of moving forward is taking up the cause which took your loved one away from you. Joining an organization that raises money and support for research for diseases can give you a purpose and determination to help find a cure so that others don't have to feel the same loss.

Speaking to groups about drunk driving, drugs, suicide prevention, the dangers of smoking, terrorism, or whatever the circumstances of your loss was, can empower you to make a difference and give you a reason to get out of bed.

Pray to find your new purpose. Then follow your heart and get out there and do it. Saving the lives of others is the best form of honoring the ones you love.

DAILY READING

> **Somebody ought to tell us, right at the start of our lives, that we are dying. Then we might live life to the limit every minute of every day. Do it, I say, whatever you want to do, do it now.**
> ***- Michael Landon***

Life has a way of flying by, doesn't it? What are some of the things you have thought about doing but haven't done yet?

Drive a race car? Write a book? Vacation in Switzerland? Work doing something you LOVE instead of the job that pays the bills but gives no satisfaction? Volunteer with children or at an animal shelter?

Make a list of things that make you feel alive. Things that make you smile. Things that will make getting out of bed easier.

Repeat out loud:

I will honor my loved one by living my life to the fullest.

My list:

_____

_____

_____

_____

_____

_____

_____

_____

_____

_____

_____

_____

_____

_____

_____

_____

_____

_____

_____

_____

_____

_____

DAILY READING

This is not the end. It is not even the beginning of the end. But, it is, perhaps, the end of the beginning.

- _Winston Churchill_

Everything is different now. Your life will keep moving past the loss. But your future will be different now. The plans you had can't be the same. It is a new beginning of your reality. It will take time to adjust your vision of life without your loved one. It will never be the same. If you have lost a spouse, you have started to live on your own. If you have lost a child, you began to live without them. By now, you are several months into that transition. It is the end of the beginning of this new way of living. Realize that you have had remarkable strength and courage to come this far. Your perseverance will enable you to create a different life than you planned. You will never forget them. You will carry them with you into this new life. Their influence on you is now tattooed into your DNA. They want you to be happy again because they love you too.

Breathe. You have passed the end of the beginning.

DAILY READING

I've learned from experience that the greater part of our happiness or misery depends on our dispositions and not on our circumstances.
Martha Washington

We all know people who are just miserable. We all also know people who seem to be happy no matter what is happening around them. Is this their disposition? Or is it a conscious mindset? Part of their personality is programmed at birth. However, we do make choices that affect our level of happiness or misery in spite of our circumstances. One person sees the glass half full; the other sees it half empty.

This is a good time to examine your own disposition. How much of your mood is affected by your choice? How do you want to feel? How do you want others to view you? What steps can you take, even with your current circumstances, to have happiness?

_____

_____

_____

_____

_____

_____

DAILY READING

**Experience is a hard teacher. She gives us
the test first, and the lessons afterwards.**
-Anonymous

If it were up to you, learning a lesson from this tragedy is the last thing you want to do. It sounds almost mean to think that our bad life experiences teach us anything valuable. However, as time passes, you will find that this experience has taught you life lessons. Your lessons will be as unique as you are. This will be another building block of wisdom. Surely you will have a different perspective after this. Looking back in your journal can bring to light some of the ways your thoughts, beliefs and emotions have changed.

What lessons have made you stronger? Wiser?

_____

_____

_____

_____

_____

_____

_____

_____

DAILY READING

> *Sometimes our fate resembles a fruit tree in winter. Who would think that those branches would turn green again and blossom, but we hope it, we know it.*
> *-Johann Wolfgang von-Goethe*

Those of us who live in areas with four seasons, take for granted that every ninety days or so, the climate will usher in a change. We never doubt that the leaves will grow again on the stark trees of winter. We have seen it happen over and over. So our belief system has formed because the pattern has been proven.

For those of us who have suffered multiple bereavements over our lives, we know for a certainty that as time moves on, our grief will lighten to allow us to lead a "normal life". Our life will be different, just as the leaves each spring are different.

Remember: The new normal will take adjustment, will ebb and flow, and will carry you forward through life's seasons.

DAILY READING

> **Unhappiness is the ultimate form of self-indulgence.**
> **-Tom Robbins, Jitterbug Perfume**

This is a new way of thinking about focusing on our negative experiences or emotions. If you re-read this quote several times, it will begin to make sense. Life itself is such a gift. When you open your eyes every day, you are privileged to spend your day making choices that can bring joy, pleasure and happiness. The aroma of your morning coffee, the warmth of a hot shower, the sight of sunshine pouring through the windows, saying "Good Morning" to the first person you see are all small details of life that can breeze by without noticing how special they are. But when you cloud your day with thoughts of what you do not have, you turn all your attention on yourself and disregard the millions of small gifts of everyday life. You also miss out on bringing joy into other's lives because you are too preoccupied with yourself.

Choose to focus today on your five senses and pleasing them to bring contentment into your life. Open yourself up to the vast world outside yourself. Smile. You have permission.

Chapter 11

SPECIAL DAYS – How to Get Through Them

HOW DO YOU get through Holidays, Anniversary of the death, Their birthday, Your birthday, Mother's Day, Father's Day, Christmas, Valentine's Day, Easter/Passover, Thanksgiving, Vacations, Wedding Anniversary and other Special Days?

You probably never noticed how many holidays and special days there are throughout the year until now. It seems that every time you turn around, there is another "special" day that you should be celebrating.

Holidays, anniversaries, and birthdays are usually wonderful days that you look forward to. Now, you may dread their arrival. How are you supposed to act?

These special days will not be the same for you or for those you love who are also grieving. It is a confusing time. Just as you may have started to live a "normal" life, their birthday, a holiday or the anniversary of their death looms in front of you. Just thinking about it can cause you to be thrust back into the depths of sorrow. You may want to try to avoid these days by hiding. It may hurt every time you go in a store and see holiday decorations, so you avoid shopping. Or you simply wish these days would pass with no mention. Realistically, you know that your mind will be thinking of your loved one no matter how much you try not to.

Friends and family may not know what to say or do. Do they have a party and invite you? If so, will you think they are disrespectful of your feelings? If they say nothing, will you think they are insensitive? If you are feeling better and they bring up the person, will you be upset?

Be reassured that everyone doesn't know what to do or how to act. There is no rule book for this. Since everyone feels differently, there is no way to know what is "right". What is right for you may feel wrong for someone else. So, how are you supposed to act?

Be true to what you are feeling and communicate it to those who care about you. Perhaps you can think of a way to honor your loved one in a way they would have liked and ask others to be a part of that day in that way.

One couple who lost their teenage son in a car accident, invited all his friends to his 18th birthday party. The mom said it was awkward at first, but when they explained to those attending that they missed seeing his friends and still wanted to be a part of their lives, it opened up a door for these young people to express their feelings of loss, tell stories of fun times together, and have a forum to feel united in friendship once again. These parents had not just lost their son. They lost the community that he was a part of. By reuniting everyone, the tension between everyone was relieved. Everyone knew that from then on, they were welcome to be a part of each other's lives and that while they all missed how things used to be, they would continue to rejoice for each other's future.

Another common reaction to special days is to become so busy that you won't have time to think. Some try to occupy themselves with cooking, gift buying, visiting, working, or whatever will fill their days to the point of exhaustion. Keep in mind that your emotions are always there, no matter how busy you are or how you try to ignore them. If you don't honor them, they will just build up until they will show up in a not so pretty way.

Realize that what you feel is okay. There is no right or wrong. Validate yourself by telling those around you how you are feeling and what you need from them. Don't allow friends or family to try to dictate how you should feel. "Should" is an expectation. People have all kinds of expectations on behavior. The only one that is true is what you are feeling inside. The only way they know what those feelings are is by communicating them. Feeling like you "should" be doing this or that, is an expectation that is untrue. Thinking you "should" be feeling a different way, is invalidating your true feelings.

If you aren't up to celebrating a holiday, say so. If you want to be around people but may get upset now and then, let them know. If you need people to allow you to cry, tell them. If you want to go to a party and dance, explain that you are honoring what your loved one would have wanted for you. Communication is the key.

How do I know what I want? Sit down by yourself and hone in on exactly how you picture yourself spending the upcoming special day. Be aware of how you feel as you envision it. When you come upon a scenario that feels right, you will know. Having a plan ahead of time will help. However, if you feel differently on that day, plans can change. Alert those around you that even though you would like to attend their function, you may need to cancel at the last minute if you aren't up to coming. They will understand and appreciate your honesty.

Also, remember that others may forget dates that are significant to you. As people go through their daily lives, they may forget the anniversary of the death, their birthday or some other special day. Don't suffer in silence. Feeling like you are the only one that remembers can be isolating and bitter. Mention the upcoming date to someone who also loved them. They may be wondering if they should mention it. Recognize if you need help and make plans with them to help you through the day. This doesn't mean you are weak or crazy. It is perfectly natural and a way to honor your heart.

Sometimes the anticipation of the special day turns out to bring more anxiety than the actual day. This is because you are trying to figure out how to handle it. Until you have a plan, your mind will wonder in every direction seeking what you "should" do. You are wondering what others will expect of you. What you expect of you. What is "normal". There is no "normal". Make a plan that settles your mind and heart, and then do it. The first holiday or anniversary will be the hardest. After that, you can tweak your plans because you will have experience in what felt good, and what didn't work for you.

Drawing close to God on these days will help you through them. Picture God or an angel hugging you.

"Trust in him at all times. Before him pour out your heart. God is a refuge for us." Psalms 62:8

For those of you who are spiritual, speaking to God and pouring out your heart can relieve the anxiety and stress of your heartbreak. Even though we can't understand death and why it happens, ask for solace from your Higher Power to bring you peace.

For those of you who do not believe in a Higher Power, reach out to someone you love to help you through these special days. Your friends and loved ones can infuse strength into your soul at a time when you need special care. Be aware that their reaction to helping you may be different than what you need or expect. Try to limit your company on these special days to those who will honor your wishes and feelings. Although you may love someone, there are those who will criticize you and make you feel worse. You know who they are. Don't feel obligated to be with them. You need warmth, comfort and compassion right now. So choose those who will fill you with these loving expressions. As you get stronger, you will be able to deal with those who choose to be negative.

Afterward

As time moves past your initial loss, may you continue to be blessed with true friends, loving family, spiritual guidance, physical strength, emotional support and peace of heart. May you find purpose in all the relationships that have become a part of who you are.

Wishing I could be with you now to give you a huge hug.

-Cindy Cipriani

Recommended Reading:

Surviving the Holidays – www.griefshare.org
Understanding Your Grief – Alan D. Wolfelt, Ph. D.
Grief and Grieving – Debra Holland, M.S., Ph.D.
Feeling Good – The New Mood Therapy – David Burns
Emotional First Aid – Gina Ross & Peter Levine

About the Author

Cindy Cipriani shares her days with her handsome husband, Jay, her too-cute-for-words goldendoodle, Lexi, and the welcome visits from three grown sons. She is the founder of Clear Path Institute, LLC with the mission of enriching the lives of those going through life transitions by providing proven step-by-step systems to simplify, sort and solve any personal or business problem in record time.

Through her own life experience, research and mentoring, Cindy has a compelling perspective on what it takes to overcome anything life can throw at you, while balancing a family and a successful career.

Using her unique 5 step process called "The 5 C Solution", your path can be simplified and put back on track during times when you need comfort, hope and direction.

Cindy would love to speak to you, your group or organization. To receive more information about Clear Path Institute's life navigation coaching, books, programs, retreats and tools, call Toll Free 1-888-806-9678. Or write to Cindy Cipriani, Clear Path Institute LLC, 665 N. Broad Street, Woodbury, NJ 08096. Visit our website: **http://clearpathinstitute.com** or send her an email: info@clearpathinstitute.com.